# Farmer's Daughter

# Farmer's Daughter

## And I Can Prove It

## Resa Willis

Acclaim Press
MORLEY, MISSOURI

Acclaim Press
— Your Next Great Book —
P.O. Box 238
Morley, MO 63767
(573) 472-9800
www.acclaimpress.com

Book Design: Rodney Atchley
Cover Design: M. Frene Melton

ISBN: 978-1-942613-78-7 | 1-942613-78-4
Library of Congress Control Number: 2017912613

First Printing: 2018
Printed in the United States of America
10 9 8 7 6 5 4 3 2 1

*This publication was produced using available information.*
*The publisher regrets it cannot assume responsibility for errors or omissions.*

# CONTENTS

# ACKNOWLEDGMENTS

I owe thanks to the organizers of my high school's 40th class reunion. I wouldn't have gone back to Iowa where I grew up if they hadn't thrown this bash and my husband, Michael, wanted to attend. Since I owe him thanks for so many things, I'll include his curiosity about American high school reunions. He was infinitely curious about my past just as I loved visiting where he grew up in England. He didn't find visiting the "olde country" so much fun, so the shoe was on the other foot. Yet the experience turned out to be as comfortable as, well, you know the comparison.

I wish I could thank every person I knew growing up in my Iowa farming community—the relatives, friends, neighbors. I owe much inspiration to Franklin and Wanda Heisterkamp who out of the blue sent me the aerial photo of my family's house, barn, machine shed, and other out buildings. All the buildings are gone now, but the land is still there, and they are farming it just as their family farmed the area when my father did.

Much thanks goes to those who know when to ask about my writing and when not to: my friends, Kathy Kurk, Eltjen Flikkema, and Carol Browning.

If you are a writer, you choose a rather lonely life sitting at a desk. If you are lucky enough to get published, you then become an author who goes out into the public arena to promote your books. I couldn't play the role of author without the people who keep me looking good inside and out: my old friends

J.D. Dunning and Linda Palmisano edit me and my work. Dr. Alice Riedel and Phyllis Stegner keep my body in working order. I can always quote Mark Twain, "I committed murder again today. Someone asked when my book would be published." Because of Acclaim Press, I didn't have to murder anyone. So thanks go to Douglas Sikes who encouraged me to publish this book. Randy Baumgardner patiently guided the book along the path to the finished product. Shirley Rash is a talented copy editor who corrected my errors. Frene Melton and Douglas Sikes designed the cover and captured the tone of my book.

As an English professor, I know the words of Thomas Wolfe, "You can't go home again." Yet, as a writer, my goal for this book was to share my "going home" experience with love and humor.

This book is dedicated to
all my city girl nieces who wanted stories
about being a farmer's daughter.

Theresa, Chelsea, Kayleigh, and Grace
Lydia and Olivia
Angela, Emily Joyce, and Rebecca

And Debbie, who is no longer here
but is always here.

# INTRODUCTION

M ark Twain wrote in his autobiography that when he was younger, "I could remember anything, whether it had happened or not...soon I shall be so I cannot remember any but the things that never happened." We all remember things differently, and this memoir is how I recall being a "farmer's daughter" growing up in Iowa in the '50s and '60s.

As a biographer I'm usually involved in the past of literary or historical figures. When I couldn't settle on a subject for another book, I thought about chronicling my own life although it is so much easier to snoop into the nooks and crannies of someone else's life. Dredging up your past isn't easy, but I found comfort in that I probably wouldn't threaten to sue myself if I read something I didn't like.

I've toyed with the idea of doing real genealogy work on my family's past. I would certainly do that on a person I was researching for a biography. What I know of my family's history as I describe it in this book is very sketchy. That is the reality I lived and how I remember it. Complete or not, my imprecise heritage is a part of me.

The people and stories in my memoir are all real. I did change names to protect the innocent, the guilty, the indifferent. As for the facts, Mark Twain also said that while facts contained poetry, "You can't use too many of them...."

I give many proofs in this book to merit my title of "farmer's daughter." The ultimate one is that I became a writer because writing like farming is pretty much a gamble. You work hard, put your product out there, but there are never any guarantees. Sometimes you get paid once a year, every other year or not at all. Still you do it, because something in your soul says this is what you must do.

# Farmer's Daughter

## And I Can Prove It

*Proof #1*

# FARM LIFE IS ALWAYS WITH ME

The great cosmic question of existence is not "What is the purpose of life?" but "Is there life after high school?" It is much debated in a multitude of self-help books, movies, songs, and even musicals. For some people, the answer is no—these are the ones who plan the high school reunions. For others the answer is yes— these are the people who avoid high school reunions.

For forty years I evaded the invitations to celebrate the passage of time from my Iowa farming community high school and my fellow fifty-six graduates to celebrate the passage of time. After all those years, I didn't want to see where my family farmed while I rode the school bus to gain an education so I could, in my father's words, "Get a good job so you won't have to depend on the land to live." When I finally looked at the rows of corn where the farmhouse had stood, I was still a farmer's daughter no matter how much I had accomplished or where I'd been. I was still the little round girl with her bad home perm, a faded print dress too tattered to wear to school with dirty legs and feet handing her father tools as he tuned the tractor.

Every five or ten years, I would receive notices decorated with balloons and streamers to attend my high school reunion. I destroyed these cheery missives to "Fellow Classmates" before my curious English husband could find them. The invitations were all issued by the same group of young women who planned every class activity from sock hops and pep rallies to class elections. Their clones have existed in every high school since the beginning of time: the prom queen, the jock, the brain, the cheerleader, the hanger-on who hoped some of the glitter of the other four would land on her shoulders by proximity. I was part of the outsiders group who preferred the Beatles to the Beach Boys and worked on the yearbook, which would celebrate the accomplishments of the social butterflies. We danced with each other after the Friday night game as the popular boys preferred the Merriment Mafia who, of course, had planned the shindig. I was friendly toward these girls, but I stayed out of their way as they rushed about with clipboards and posters. It took them forty years before this in-crowd who planned their schoolmates' lives got the best of me. Obviously, they had bribed my mailman to get the latest invitation into my husband's hands before I got to the mailbox.

My husband was schooled in classrooms under portraits of Her Majesty while I sat in classrooms under unfinished portraits of George Washington. When he opened an envelope and confetti sprinkled onto the floor, I knew I was going back to Iowa. Like an anthropologist invited to observe an unknown tribe, he began to plan the trip. He wanted to experience this nostalgic, yet masochistic American ritual. I had kept him ignorant of these festivities for years when others he knew would be attending their class reunions. "Does your class ever have such gatherings?" he would ask sweetly. He knew I had attended a twenty-year reunion with my niece who had, considering my graduating class numbers, a massive graduation class of around 300. I had gone as a type of reunion guerrilla operative. I convinced many there that I had graduated with them with such phrases as "I sat behind you in Mr. Urbey's math class" or "Remember that assembly when Tommy sang that song about the girl who threw herself in the river?"

I made my husband watch the movie *Romy and Michelle's High School Reunion*, and he still wanted to go. When he saw me filling out the required questionnaire, he asked in disbelief, "They actually make you do that?" "Yes," I replied, "That's why I've been avoiding reunions for years." Besides the standard inquiries—"Where do you work and what do you do," and about children and grandchildren—there were more imaginative ones such as "What is your funniest memory from high school?"

As a testament to my high school experience, I couldn't think of one funny moment except when Tommy sang that song at assembly, but that had never happened. When asked about what I'd done that was noteworthy, I couldn't help myself. I quoted Romy and Michelle—I had invented Post-Its. "You did not," said my husband, "but you look cute when you lie." You gotta love a man who still thinks you're cute when you're over sixty. I was going to my high school reunion. As a literature teacher, I knew all about the wisdom of trying or not trying to "go home again." My body had left after graduation, but the values were planted in my heart on an Iowa farm. I was still a farmer's daughter and the way I had lived my life proved it.

*My paternal grandparents*

# FARM LIFE IS HARD WORK

My high school reunion took place in a one-room community center that had been built after I'd left the region. It housed a kitchen and floor-to-ceiling partitions so the one large room could be divided into smaller ones. It was about a block from the high school on Main Street, which was pretty much the only street. A few side lanes branched past the high school with empty, decaying houses outnumbering the inhabited ones. Just about the entire town's population of 400 lived not in the town but near it on farmland.

The community center was one of the few serviceable buildings. Main Street bustled when I was at school. Once the school bus passed the four grain elevators and bumped over the train tracks dissecting the edge of town, you'd go by Benson's Grocery Store, Hugh's Gas Station and Garage, the Koffee Kup Kafe, and assorted offices of insurance agents, a staple to any farm district due to the precarious business of farming. No farmer ever had to go to Las Vegas. It was enough of a gamble trying to outwit the weather, and the house usually won. The post office was in the bank building as the bank had closed during the Depression. Past the high school and at the other end of Main Street, churches presided for each of the big three Protestant denominations:

Methodist, Baptist, Presbyterian. You had to go to a larger town to worship as a Catholic, Episcopalian or Latter Day Saint. If you needed to buy a new car, truck or farm equipment such as a tractor, grain combine or plow, or of lesser importance, clothes and shoes, you headed to a larger town, one with a population of 3000 and usually a half-hour drive away. After 1963 when "liquor by the drink" became legal, the same went for a bar. If you were in the midst of planting or harvesting and couldn't leave the farm, you ordered by mail from the Sears, Penney's or Montgomery Ward catalogs, the original online shopping.

After forty years the grocery store was an antique swap meet place with a bear carved by a chainsaw standing guard out front. Dusty lamp shades, a Brady Bunch lunch box and, of all things, a cricket bat identified handily by my husband adorned the windows. The world is a smaller place now. My friend Diane Benson and her family had lived over the grocery store. For me, sleepovers there were intriguing as giggly girls could just scurry down the steps from the living quarters, switch on the lights of the closed store, and pull potato chips and cookies off the shelves or ice cream out of the freezer. Leave your purse at home—no money required.

My cousin's gas station and one bay garage had been replaced by a convenience chain, which probably sold more candy bars and donuts than anything. Other buildings had boarded up broken glass windows. The four-lane highway had made it too easy to go to bigger towns for fast food, malls, movie theaters and jobs. Many in my graduating class still lived in the radius of the town but worked in one of the big cities fifty miles to the north and south for the two big employers of the area, insurance and communications.

Of the fifty-six graduates of my class who had been found, thirty-six of them still lived in the area. Seventeen of us had moved away. No wonder the reunion could boast an attendance of half the graduating class. The five party planners had all gone to the big city and met constantly since graduation to continue their social consciousness. They threw the first class reunion only five years after we received our diplomas. Just a week after I was trying to forget the reunion I had just attended, a letter showed up in my mail box with the opening, "Well, guess what we are starting to plan?"

After the banquet of rubber chicken and shoe leather roast beef, we were asked to stand and talk about what everyone had been doing the past forty years. I always cautioned my students to be thorough but brief when asked to speak about themselves. "We care, but we don't care that much." This caveat was not delivered to this group. My table went early. I stood up and said my name and words to the effect, "Here's my husband; I live in Missouri. I'm a teacher and a writer."

Not having attended past reunions, I didn't know what to expect. Others must have known this portion of the program was coming because they were prepared to relive their lives. "My name is Lucy Conyers. After I graduated I went to work for the Consolidated Telephone Company. I started as an operator and within six months I had worked my way up to rolling up the telephone cords for the repairmen. I left in 1968 to work for the Black Mask and Gun Insurance Company. In 1970 I got married, but my first husband left me when I became pregnant with triplets. I now refer to them as the twins as I am estranged from one of the triplets. He didn't like my fourth husband. We haven't spoken in six years." On and on it went. Too many droned the year by year experiences of their lives and capped it off with encores of praise of their grandchildren as the cutest, cleverest ever born.

My ears hurt. My husband's stiff upper lip quivered. I zoned out except to notice that at least seven there were farmers or farmers' wives. I was heartened to think that some were still working their family farms. When I think of my father and mother, I think of one word: work. I didn't know my parents very long. When I was seventeen and about to graduate, my father didn't wake up one morning. He died of a heart attack. My mother lasted barely a year after his death before she succumbed to a brain tumor. I have now lived longer than both of them and my older two sisters.

My recollections of my parents are of them driving tractors, feeding livestock, canning vegetables. They never took vacations, seldom went to the movies or watched television. They were up with the sun and kept going until it was dark. When it was night or the weather was bad and you couldn't get into the fields, there were always outbuildings to keep up, cows to be milked, clothes or equipment mending to be done, records to be kept. You worked or you ate or you slept. No one needed to worry about filling time. There was always something to be done. Observing their ceaseless activities, no wonder to this day I feel strangely guilty watching a reality television show. Shouldn't I have graded papers, emptied the dishwasher, or castrated some pigs?

My earliest memory is of sitting in the front seat of our 1950 Ford named Fancy. She was parked at the end of a row of just-planted corn. I watched my mother drive a Farmal tractor up and down, eight tilled rows at a time. Today tractors can plant up to thirty-two rows at a time with enclosed cabs for air conditioning and satellite radio. My mother's air conditioning was an overlarge umbrella fastened to the back of the tractor. It was spring in Iowa and time to plant the corn if it was to be "knee high by the Fourth of July." My father was planting in another field. He hadn't become a mechanized farmer until World War II. All of his life he maintained that if you wanted to plow a truly straight row in a field you needed a horse or a mule.

I was surrounded by books and my doll LuLu who was "married" to my stuffed monkey, Zack. For a snack I had a thermos of milk and black square devil's food cookies. Today I have to rush past the cookie aisle in the grocery store because I can still taste them. My mother would come to the end of the row, turn the tractor around, smile and wave, and slowly grow smaller as I watched her cultivate the next set of rows. I wasn't in school yet so I was probably about three or four. My daycare was that car. Who could babysit me when all the neighbors were in the fields?

My parents farmed 600 acres in western Iowa close to the Missouri River. All of our few neighbors were farmers, everyone we knew farmed or was connected on the edge of it supplying goods and services to the farmers. The number one topic of conversation was always the weather as it could make or break you. Too much rain, not enough, hail, the possibility of tornadoes, bad storms.

It wasn't until I was in college and my parents both dead that I realized that my father had been a sharecropper. Half of his earnings from his crops had gone to the owner of the property as rent. Any livestock, eggs, milk, or garden products he sold were our "mad money." He, of course, had to buy and maintain all of his own farm equipment and vehicles. We weren't rich, but we never lacked for anything. My mother would often declare, "Your father would be a rich man if his family wasn't always sponging off of him." I didn't dare ask what she meant. I just had to accumulate facts over time about this mystery statement.

The only farm I knew was the one on which I grew up. I did hear my family talk about the "old place" across the river. When my older sisters came home, they would often request to go look at the "old place." I never visited it, but I learned there were no longer buildings there. What had the house been like? Why were the buildings gone? Why had my family moved? I never asked those questions then as I'm sure I was at first too young to care and later too self involved to care. Now I have no one to ask.

I realized my parents did not own their house or the land from an early age because already busy times would get more hectic when the "landlady" was coming to visit. Her name was Cora Jane. She and her husband lived in Omaha, a big city on a hill far away. Today, it is only about fifty miles away. Her father was very wealthy and owned most of western Iowa. He left the running of his farms to his daughter and her husband. The land had been secured by his father who had come from Germany at the age of fourteen and made his fortune in banking and then bought land. I knew as much about my grandfather as I did about our landlady's grandfather. My paternal grandfather had also come from Germany at a young age, but he had never made any type of fortune. I never knew him; like my maternal grandparents he had died before I was born. I assume he was also a farmer, but I never heard my parents say. In a few surviving photos in the old shoebox that houses these treasures, he looks tired and sad. He died, as my father would, at the age of sixty.

Everything had to be spick and span for the landlady's visits in the spring and fall, planting and harvesting time. After the windows were washed, the grass mowed, my collie Ring brushed, the tires of a big new Cadillac would crunch down our driveway.

I knew she had to be rich. The car was usually pink, just like Elvis drove or sometimes white. My father would always remark that they got a new car every year. That was true wealth to him as we got a new car only every ten years if times were good. When I was little, Cora Jane would sit on the floor with me and play with my dolls and toys. When I got older and got off the school bus, she would ask what I was doing at school. She gave me the princessly sum of $100 when I graduated from high school in 1967, and she sent me a silver platter when I got married.

She served as my first example of a stylish, well-educated, successful woman in a man's world. Her hair was perfectly coiffed, her hands immaculate, her nails polished when she removed her gloves, and she wore mascara and lipstick. Yet, she was never prissy. She would energetically follow my father around in her high heels as she inspected hogs and cows or climbed into the battered pickup to journey out to the fields. When I was old enough to read *Vogue,* I realized she wore real Chanel suits. Later, I admired Jackie Kennedy. She also had coiffed hair, nice jewelry, and Chanel suits, but I don't know if she ever admired a cow with a nursing calf. My poor mother knew of nicer things beyond crops and livestock from reading popular magazines, but they did not fit the lifestyle of her roles as farmhand, wife and mother. My mother could never afford such luxuries, wouldn't know where to buy them if she could or have the opportunity to wear them, except to church functions. Imagine a pillbox hat, gloves, and a Chanel suit at the Wesleyan Ladies Society in the basement of the Methodist church.

My mother would make homemade bread and a special elaborate dessert such as coconut cream pie or German chocolate cake from scratch, no box mixes. A chicken or a piglet laid down its life so Cora Jane and spouse could eat lunch or supper with us and then go off to visit her other farms in the area or as my husband would later remark, "Like a queen on a progress." I suppose so, but she and her husband were kind and granted the modest requests my parents asked for: repairs to the barn roof, another corn crib to store a bountiful crop. When I was around 12, our landlady remodeled the farmhouses she owned with indoor bathrooms. Until then, you got to take a leisurely stroll to the outhouse between the wash house where my mother did the laundry and the cellar that stored our home canned goods. At night there was the pot under the bed. It built character or maybe just made you regular.

My father's mantra was that if you worked hard at school, something he'd never had much of an opportunity to do, you could get a good job and not have to work as hard as a farmer. I would have been disowned if I had married a farmer instead of planning for college.

I didn't realize that my father's hard work had made him successful until his death. I heard friends and neighbors repeat how he was the best farmer in the area, how he knew the most about the land. I heard stories of how he'd helped others with advice or loaning equipment or giving of his time and money. Our landlady remarked succinctly, "No one knew his craft as Lawrence did." For me, he was just always busy, but he was always happy.

I learned from farm life that life is hard work, but it can pay off. You can support yourself and your family. There is a satisfaction in doing something well and seeing the results of it. You can count on work however you define it. It never leaves you. You can take refuge in it no matter what else is happening in your life. Maybe work is an obsession too, but it is more fulfilling than drugs or alcohol.

I remember a sermon from my childhood church years. The minister said the first act of God was work and creativity—he created the heavens and the earth. God also gave Adam work to do—to multiply and replenish the earth. Another of Adam's first acts was of work and of language—he named the animals. Things went down hill from there. He should have just stuck with the hard work or, like me, became an English major.

*My parents at a young age*

*Proof #3*

# FARM LIFE VALUES EDUCATION

F ew in my graduating class had been in my kindergarten class. Joey and Karen were my closest friends when the state "consolidated" the school districts. No longer would each small town have its own grade school, junior high, and high school. One town would use its school buildings for the lower grades; a neighboring town would handle freshmen through seniors. Joey, Karen, and I started together and ended together. I really wanted to see Karen, but she didn't attend the class reunion. I guess, unlike me, she didn't have to prove her love to anyone by attending.

Because we consolidated into a larger school district, the "rich" kids tried to make us feel inferior by saying such things as "Do they have electricity in your town?" It was gratifying to have Joey whisper to me, "Isn't it nice to know that we 'poor river rats' have more education than the others in this room?" He knew how we'd been taunted for living a few miles closer to the Sioux River than the town where we attended high school, which was just closer to the highway and the county seat. Such distinctions human beings as eternal adolescents love to make. Joey was now a medical doctor and I'm, in my nephew's words, the kind of doctor who doesn't do anyone any good. I have a Ph.D.

My parents would have been pleased at Joey's insight. They stressed education so much because they had only gone through the eighth grade. That's not to say they weren't intelligent. They were well read. In bad weather and if they were caught up on their chores, they saw it as a duty to read and learn. They took me to the local Carnegie Library. I used to stare at the portrait of Andrew Carnegie over the library's fireplace. I thought he lived upstairs, and he let me check out his books. In a sense he did. Years later when I wrote about Mark Twain, I was happy that Carnegie was a friend of his. It made us all closer somehow.

My father taught me to read before I went to school. I would sit on his lap as he held a small blackboard on which he would write and I would write by copying his patterns. I could count and write numbers. I could say and write the alphabet. Somehow my dad had copies of the Dick and Jane books. He had probably gotten them from my oldest sister who had been a teacher before she "retired" at the age of twenty-four and got married. My father would read the lines aloud, "See Spot run" and I would "read" them, too. It wasn't Dostoevsky, but I could read simple things years before I was formally taught to read.

My parents had many books, hardback books. I don't know where they came from as there were no bookstores within a hundred miles. They weren't lightweight tomes, either, but editions of Shakespeare, Austen, Melville, poetry, and plays. No wonder I became an English professor and a writer. They also kept up with contemporary literature. That triumvirate of magazines that graced most homes in the '50s and '60s, *Life, Look, The Saturday Evening Post* would run installments of the latest novels of Steinbeck, Hemingway, Fitzgerald, Faulkner. My parents would save up the magazines until they had the completed novel and then read the entire book.

My first career choice was to be a librarian because I loved organizing and reorganizing the books housed in our spare bedroom. When I later learned that being a librarian did not involve being paid to read, I lowered my sights. I still revere librarians greatly as guardians of knowledge.

As I grew older and could read more, I began to notice that my parents might be reading books I had not catalogued in my library. One afternoon as my mother was working in the vegetable garden, I got to snooping around. Ah, ha! Some books were hidden under the sheets at the bottom of the closet in the spare bedroom. *Lady Chatterley's Lover, Peyton Place, The Tropic of Cancer.* It was obvious that these were the sweetest of fruits—forbidden! Of course, I wanted to read them. I would sneak a look at these masterpieces when my parents were occupied elsewhere. You can't fool mothers. Somehow she found out and began putting other books in there—Chaucer's *The Canterbury Tales*, Boccacio's *The Decameron*, Dante's *The Divine Comedy*—books where you really had to look to find the smut. I was even expected to learn from the illicit.

State legislators sold consolidation to Iowans with the promise of more money for superior schools: additional educational opportunities, better-trained teachers, extra funds for basketball, football and wrestling teams, all dear to Iowa hearts. Things seemed the same to me except I had a much longer bus ride. I had to leave earlier, and I got home later often missing *American Bandstand.* Damn.

When I was in kindergarten, my bus ride, which picked up students in the morning and dropped them off in the afternoon, was about a half hour each way. When I was in high school, my riding time had nearly tripled. No one wanted to spend more time with Old Man Titch than was necessary.

Farmers often drove bus routes for extra money. One of my father's brothers drove a route for years. Uncle Harvey was easygoing, and I could imagine that he drove the bus as he drove a tractor, in his own world shutting out the kid noises emanating from behind him. You could pass the time on his bus by listening to your transistor radio if you kept it low or had earplugs, talking with your friends, or studying if you had a test scheduled. Old Man Titch, despite that he had no teeth, probably hadn't yet earned the title of "old man." For a kid, everyone over thirty is "old." When I was in grade school, he had false teeth that used to project out of his mouth when he yelled at his passengers. "Turn off that radio! How can you listen to that crap?!" If you tried to lean out of your seat and talk to someone a distance from you, you heard, "Sit down and shut up, you hoods." Out flew his teeth; laughter entailed from us hooligans. By the time I was in junior high, he had given up wearing the falsies. No wonder. The state of dental arts at that time couldn't have been much of an art or a science. Distance makes me realize that driving a school bus would be a talent that I could no more practice than waiting tables or doing surgery. These professions take skills and a patience that I could never possess. Titch was also caretaker of the town cemetery, where he replaced plastic wreaths that had blown off the graves and he mowed the grass.

On rainy days or in the winter, at the rare times when farmers got caught up on their work, they spent their time in the barber shop getting haircuts but more importantly, talking. My mother's church group gossiped, but farmers in a barbershop discussed the state of the world. According to my father, Titch would set forth disparaging all politicians, his fellow townsfolk, and the brats on his bus route, of course.

To an adult audience he referred to all of us "little bastards." He would end his tirade by commentating on the previous barber, Floyd. Yes, Floyd just like on the *Andy Griffith Show*. There must be a cosmic rule that if you are named Floyd you will become a barber. If you name your children Floyd, immediately enroll them in barber school. Their fates have been cast.

Floyd had gone to his "reward," the barbershop in the sky, to be replaced by Ray. Floyd had had the audacity to ban Titch from the barbershop because of what is now called negative energy. Back then he was just crabby. Titch had the last word on Floyd at rest in the cemetery, "I give him better haircuts than he ever gave me."

Riding the school bus was an education in itself. I had to be ready with my books and coat on the bed as I looked out my bedroom window to watch for the yellow bus. Iowa is flat, and you could see any vehicle from a distance. When the bus was on the bridge, I put on my coat, picked up my books, and walked out the door to the top of our driveway. The bus would stop, Titch would swing open the big door, and I climbed on board. I said, "Good Morning" to him at my mother's insistence although I had to endure the groans from the passengers already on the bus. I didn't dare forego greeting him because my mother, with her magical mother powers, would find out. He grunted and watched me in his rearview mirror as I moved down the aisle to sit with my friend Ginny on the seats above the back wheels. Those were our favorites as you could put your feet on the wheelbase and rest them there. Once I was seated, he started to move the bus. If you had ever given him a problem, he sometimes took off as you made your way to your seat. He reserved this treatment for the older boys who liked to congregate in the back where they bragged about romantic conquests they never made and took the bus seats apart. Sometimes they would pull their leather jackets over their heads and sleep because of their pressing social lives or having to get up early and do farm chores before getting ready for school. Titch called them "hoods" or "greasers," the young farm versions of Marlon Brando or Elvis Presley. When this group started sporting Beatle haircuts later, they were still "greasers" to him.

Most kids would be standing at their pickup points ready to board the bus. I bet you could ask any school bus driver in the world, and he or she will tell you there is always one who makes you wait. Ronnie was Titch's curse. Titch would lay on the horn a full half mile or so as he rounded the bend and moved toward Ronnie's house. When he reached the driveway and even before a full stop, Titch would start muttering to himself, "Sonofabitch. Why the hell can't that kid haul his ass out here? Didn't he hear the horn? How the hell can you miss a goddamn big yellow school bus?" The bus would sit outside of Ronnie's house as Titch would "beep, beep, beep" the horn. Eventually, Ronnie would appear in the door buttoning his shirt, putting on his jacket. He would leisurely stroll toward the bus eating a piece of toast or a doughnut. Often his mother would run after him and hand him his lunch or a book he had forgotten in his haste to get to the bus. You can bet that Titch slammed the bus door behind the ass that Ronnie couldn't haul and took off before he got close to a seat.

Titch was particularly solicitous to the three Peggy Sues who got on close to town and school. They were seniors. Even the greasers momentarily stopped dismantling the bus to watch them board. Wafts of perfume preceded their tittering entrance, as they stayed focused on their conversation. Ponytails, a kerchief at the neck, bobby socks, saddle shoes. They were the epitome of 1950s fashion. They wore tight little sweater tops that encased their pointed boobs. The pièce de résistance of their ensembles were the poodle skirts with all the crinoline slips that made the skirts stick out and block the aisle of the bus. Sometimes they had to turn sideways to get on the bus. What the males particularly waited for was that the girls could never just sit in a seat with those skirts and slips. They would twirl several times, as much as you could in the bus, before landing on the seat. You might just see a knee. I begged my mother for such a slip. I hoped it would make me look like them. When I did get a modified version of such apparel, I looked like a junior square dancer. My mother deemed it too frivolous to wear to school. She was probably just embarrassed, so I put it under my Blue Bird uniform. "Does my skirt stick out?" I would ask my mother over and over again as if anyone at a church club meeting for preteen girls would care.

My friend Ginny and I thought the Peggy Sues were so "cool." Ginny even asked for their autographs. It was a great bother to them, but they did sign her book. That was probably the height of their celebrity. After graduation, I'm sure they worked as secretaries in the big city for awhile and then got married.

Even cooler was Joey's mother. I admired her because when we were in the early grades, she was finishing her high school diploma. She had dropped out probably to have Joey. When he and his brother were old enough to be in school, she had gone back. When she crossed that stage in the school gymnasium to collect her diploma, the crowd cheered. In spite of a difficult marriage, being a single mom when no one was, Vicki finished her high school degree in an era when if you left school you didn't go back. From my second grade classroom, I would see her in her June Cleaver dress and high heels carrying her books as she climbed the stairs to where the "big kids" had classes. I would see her pass by again around 11:00 as she went to work in the kitchen. After lunch and cleanup, she went back upstairs for her afternoon classes. When our class was finished in the afternoon, she was there with a smile to walk home with Joey and his younger brother. They did their homework together. How she must have cheered when her son graduated from medical school.

*My father with his mules*

*Proof #4*

# FARM LIFE IS SEX

S o how many of these blokes courted you?" asked
my husband. The dreaded question, not because
I had been so pursued, but because I had been so in-
visible to the opposite sex. The odds looked good. Out
of my graduating class of fifty-six, the male persua-
sion numbered twenty-nine. If you look at the senior
photographs in the yearbook, of which I was the editor, the young men look pretty good in their coats and
ties if you knew how they looked every day in their
jeans, madras shirts and bad teeth. The females look
equally fetching even the ones with spotty complex-
ions and wiry hair in real life, airbrushed out in the
final proofs. That's why we paid all that money for
senior pictures, before glamour shots.

Senior photos today look like professional photo
shoots for *Vanity Fair* with subjects leaning on cars,
at zoos with tigers, or in dramatic dance poses with
background characters who seem to belong with
Cirque de Soleil. All of our photos were head and
shoulder shots. I searched for my dress with the flat-
tering face-framing lace for weeks in the few dress
stores in our area and ended up ordering it from the
catalog of my old standby couturier, the House of
Penn'ey. Other young ladies opted for off the shoulder
drapes that could be colored to a shade of your choice.
Senior pictures were black and white, but you could
spend big bucks and get one color-tinted version by

which to commemorate your youth and vigor at eighteen. My parents had been shocked that my packet of wallet photos, a few 5 x 7 shots and my big colored photo would cost a hefty $80. But what could you do? Like the class ring, which still fits me and there are few things I can say that about, it was a right of passage. You had to trade photos with everyone in your class as well as include a wallet size photo to everyone on the family Christmas card list, and both of my parents had more brothers and sisters than you could count on both hands, as well as all of our neighbors.

My senior photo was the hot button that caused a feud between my mother and me. My mother approved of my dress, but hated my hair. It was long and straight like any other trendy girl in the '60s. I'm sure her mother must have hated Mom's hair at some point growing up, but as with so many mother/daughter relationships, Mom had developed amnesia about it. "You can't have hair like that in your senior picture. You look like a savage. You have to get it cut and get a perm." All of my school years, until I matured into high school and absolutely refused on threats that I'd quit school and marry a farmer, I got my hair cut and permed before I would start school in the fall. I have year after year of frizzy-haired school pictures and toothy grins, with more teeth as I got older. Each school picture was more hideous than the last. School photos were taken in the fall. They lined you up in the gym, whisked you into a chair without benefit of mirror or comb, ran a string from the camera to your chin, and flash. "Next please." Six weeks later you got that one photo and an order blank to be returned with money in a few days. My God, your eyes might be closed, you might be sneering, your hair could be, and usually was, sticking up. This is how you would be immortalized in the Christmas cards sent to friends and relatives, and worst, in the school yearbook. At least with senior pictures, the photographer would take many shots, and you could pick the best. And my mother wanted me to relive the horror of grade school photography! My father noticed after a week or so that my mother and I weren't talking but doing a lot of slamming of doors, books, pots and pans. "Now girls, what's wrong?" His solution was Solomonesque. I would go to the beauty shop and have my hair put up. And where is that controversial portrait today? I have no idea. I hadn't looked at the class yearbook until I began prepping for the class reunion. After forty years, I was afraid I wouldn't remember names and faces. Once at the reunion I saw my photograph way too much. A slide program kept flashing the senior pictures on the wall. Spouses were given a button to wear with the senior photo and name of their better half. My husband, who would not be caught dead in a shirt with an alligator, polo pony, or someone's name on it, proudly walked about with my senior picture on his lapel.

Statistics would say that there would be some gay guys in my class, but I can't think of any who were on the edge of fashion or wanted to pile my hair on top of my head. I can look back and wonder about some of our female athletes who could not have cared less about their clothes or their hair. The closet was really locked tight in those days. I didn't know much about homosexuals. I'm sure they were around, but then what I knew about straight sex came from observing farm animals. If you live on a farm, you know about sex—bull on cow, boar on sow, stallion on mare, rooster on chicken, etc. You see the love making and you see the results: calves, piglets, foals, chicks. It doesn't take much of a leap of imagination to apply the observations and results to human beings.

I knew all about sex but nothing about dating. What I knew about teen dating I learned from watching *American Bandstand*, Elvis movies or Frankie and Annette beach movies, *The Patty Duke Show*. According to these sources, if you were a teenage girl you had a boyfriend who might on rare occasions kiss you to prove his devotion. He was there to talk to you, walk you to school—which would have been a long hike for my boyfriend—be nice to your parents. and take you to the game on Friday night and to the movies on Saturday night and then to the malt shop. You were both asexual, except that occasional kiss, until you got married. You went steady, a precursor to engagement and marriage one day. At my school the girl would wear the boy's class ring to signify that she was taken. Of course, the boy's ring was too big, so it was decoratively taped to fit. Sometimes thick, fluffy yarn was wrapped around the band. The ring appeared to be surrounded by a fuzzy halo.

I had no dating experience but as a good student, I studied up on it to be ready for when my time would come. I read *Seventeen, Datebook* and other teen girl tracts that had articles about what to do if a boy just couldn't control his hormones. It was up to the young ladies to keep everything above the waist and the breasts. I memorized the advice. "Put your purse on the car seat between you and him." The fashion was to sit smashed up against the boy as he drove. Seat belts would eventually make this advice archaic. If the young gentleman got "handy," put his hand aside and say, "That's not the message I'm sending, and all the lines are busy." How naïve it sounds now.

I was pleasant enough looking in high school. I was smart, and I could be fun. I got along with everyone. Yet, despite my husband's certainty that the male classmates couldn't resist me, I didn't have a boyfriend or didn't even came close to worrying about putting wool around a big ring. Of course, the reunion planners had all the parties and, except for two in the group, all the fuzzy rings. I had one real date in four years asked by someone who ignored me at the reunion. In high school he'd been a good student, an athlete and handsome with a rugged cleft chin. Now he had a mullet and didn't seem to remember me. I'm not even sure why he had asked me to his brother's birthday party. He drove a whole twenty miles from his house to pick me up and return to his parents' home. I put my purse between us on the bench seat of his father's car and practiced the lines in my head about busy signals. He drove me home, walked me to the door, and we talked while I was waiting for him to try to kiss me. He didn't although I had avoided potato chips and sour cream dip as my mother said it would give me bad breath. My mother bragged to my Aunt Nellie the next day, "Reese Ann went on her first date with a boy in a car." Maybe there was hope for me after all. A week or so later I got a letter in the mail that we should break up. Break up? He then took up with a younger woman, a sophomore. They were in marching band together. You just can't trust a musician.

I did all the high school things of going to games and dancing in the gym in my socks afterwards on Friday nights. But I went with my girlfriends, and we all danced together. That worked until there was a slow dance. The lights would go down and the steady couples wrapped themselves around each other as if having sex standing up until a faculty chaperon pulled them apart. My girlfriends and I would stand under the basketball hoop waiting for the fast songs to reconvene. On occasion, Jimmy would ask me to dance. He was smitten with me in that universal conundrum that we don't like those who like us. Love can stink.

I didn't know too much about him, only that he came from a very large, poor family. He wore the same clothes every day. His shoes had holes in them. He was the eldest of I don't know how many siblings. They moved too fast to count them. His father had taken off and the only social services in those days came from your neighbors. My mother's church group regularly collected food and clothing for the family, and I was admonished that people are proud. I was to say nothing about it to anyone. I didn't have to. All of Jimmy's brothers and sisters kept coming up to me and thanking me and my mother for the new duds and the canned goods. That's probably why he danced with me. At the reunion, he remained a mystery. All that was known was he hadn't left the area, and, sadly, he had died the day before. After the reunion, I received a class photo of all of us who had attended the festivities. In a ghostly coincidence, there on the wall behind us was Jimmy's senior photo.

The one time you absolutely had to have a date was for the spring prom. If you didn't have a date, mothers swung into action soliciting the services of long lost cousins. Even if couples broke up, they were expected to bury the hatchet and attend the prom together. Even after my messy breakup with Mr. Mullet, I didn't expect him to ask me to the prom. He had a new love and a broken leg. Sometimes the universe gives us little rewards.

My girlfriend Ginny was a year older and a graduating senior when I was a junior. Only juniors and seniors could attend the prom. Ginny always had a boyfriend and was going to marry each of them until something would happen, a breakup would ensue, and she had to find a new potential husband. Her present

soon-to-be ex worked in Omaha and had a friend for
me. His name was Phil. Phil had a catchphrase he
repeated from a popular television comedy show. He
began just about every sentence with "Would you believe...?" It still annoys me after all these years. Poor
Phil. He was used so I could fulfill my junior year fan-
tasy. I could buy a long dress, dye shoes to match,
wear a corsage, and dance at a prom.

At least my dating disasters kept me chaste. I
knew the consequences of sex. I had seen it every-
where on the farm. That's why there are the old jokes
about farmers' daughters and traveling salesmen.
Sexual activity is at orgy level for farm animals. No
one blushed at remarks about livestock penises or females in heat, but the curtain fell over any discussion
of the sexual activities of two-legged farm occupants
until some transgression became public.

Pregnancy is public. It is proof that a man and a
woman had sex. It could be the subject of great gossip about the fuzzy ring couples. Were they doing it?
Clint, who was a big brash linebacker on the football
team, began his sharing of his life after high school
at the reunion dinner, "I think you all remember that
Kim and I got married right after graduation. I bet
you were disappointed as you counted on your fingers that nine months later we didn't have a kid. We
waited four years for that, and we're still married." I
would have applauded him if he hadn't used it as a
transition into the liturgy of angelic grandchildren.

One of the styles of the '60s was a high waisted em-
pire dress a la Jane Austen. I thought they looked so
"fab" in the magazines. After all, Beatle girlfriends
wore them. As much as I wanted one of these dresses,
I knew that wearing it to school would have elicited
such comments as "When is the baby due?" It would
have had to have been an immaculate conception.

For each of the four years that I was in high school, some girl got "in trouble" and was whisked away by her parents to live with some relative in another state or county, at least. She would return to class a year later with a new baby sister or brother to be raised by her parents. And what happened to the father? Everyone knew who he was, but few said anything. He continued on in his classes and his sports team. Sometimes the soon-to-be new parents got married. This scandal occurred with my cousin Sharon, the daughter of one of my mother's sisters. Attending the hasty wedding was not an option for me, but I listened carefully to the details from my mother and Aunt Nellie. "Esther really had her cinched in. She didn't look expecting at all." When the bundle of shame was born, my Aunt Esther continued the charade, "These premature babies need such care." My mother and Aunt Nellie would look at each other and roll their eyes. I can only imagine their responses to the girls I see today who openly admire each others' expanding bumps under tight fitting clothes as they walk into their high school buildings with the "baby daddy."

I know my parents had sex three times, my two older sisters and me. And there was quite a spread among us. My oldest sister, Edith, was twenty-four when I came along. She was married and had her first baby three months after I was born. My middle sister, Janyce, was sixteen when I was born. I never saw my parents kiss, hug, or hold hands. I never heard them say, "I love you." I also never saw them argue. I guess they did all that when I wasn't around. I saw them work, talk, and often laugh. Granted, Iowans may not be known as great lovers as we tend to be modest folks, but I didn't know married couples could be affectionate until I observed some of the parents of my girlfriends. I thought kissing or calling someone "dear" or "darling" was something you only saw in the movies. Television was pretty innocent then also. It was controversial for the very married Lucy Ricardo to be pregnant as she and Ricky only ever slept in twin beds. Out of my developing romantic interests, I once asked my mother, "Why did you get married?" I'll never forget her reply. I thought I'd hear, "Because I loved your father." I didn't question their devotion to each other, but her answer to my question was "Because I wanted to leave home." I didn't ask for details. I knew she'd say, "Keep that sass for those kids in school, young lady." She had let me peek beyond the veil as much as she would allow. Any more questions and she would have slapped me.

What I did surmise from overheard conversations between Mom and Aunt Nellie was that their father had been a harsh disciplinarian. They had great affection for their grandfather, the Irishman who'd come to America. He could sing and dance jigs and left milk out for leprechauns. Besides Aunt Nellie, my mother had four other living sisters and one who had died as a young adult. She had four full brothers and a half brother. Things changed when her mother died and her father remarried. They had a new baby, Sid. Mom and Aunt Nellie reinforced what I would later read in endless literary patterns. They hated their new "mother" whose name was Dell. Her son, Sid, got everything he wanted which couldn't have been much with all of those children. My mother and my aunts were becoming young women. Perhaps my grandfather was concerned about their growing sexuality, and perhaps, they were rebelling. As usually is the case, I'm sure it was both. I remember the tale that Mom and her sisters had gone to a dance. I sat mesmerized. My mother and my aunts danced?! With young men?! "Remember, Bert?" laughed Aunt Nellie. "He'd grab your hand and hold it straight up in the air and dance you backwards and that's what he called the turkey trot!" Where did they go to this dance? Apparently, there had been a band. Even someone as sophisticated as I only danced to records. At my infamous prom despite much weeping and wailing from the graduates, the faculty picked a live band still doing turkey trot tunes. No Monkees or Motown tunes for them.

The story went on. My mother and aunts had missed their curfew. When they approached the front porch, there stood their father with a shotgun. I'm sure their high spirits stopped abruptly. "Didn't you hear me fire shots in the air?" Silence. Then my Aunt Nellie bravely said, "Why would you say that? We didn't hear anything." My mother looked at me and said, "See, you should always tell the truth. He hadn't fired the gun. If we had said he had, it would have been the strap." Maybe he brandished the gun because he didn't want to hold it to some young man's back later.

I have never seen photographs of my maternal grandparents or my leprechaun-loving great-grandfather; let alone know much about them. Because I came along "later in life," all those relatives were dead. I vaguely remember my father's mother. I only knew the brothers and sisters of my parents who lived close to us. As a group, they didn't talk much about the past. Now I feel so ignorant about my family history. I wish I'd followed Aunt Nellie's example and asked some questions and, more than that, demanded some answers.

*My father in a more mechanized era*

# FARM LIFE IS FAMILY LIFE

S ex leads to children, children lead to families, and families keep secrets. I had learned this on the farm, but I hadn't really recognized it until Sonya from my graduating class asked me, "Why do you write biographies?" She raised her eyebrows and smiled when I said, "I like finding out why people do the things they do."

Sonya had joined our class midway through the junior year. She avoided any of the cliques, which gave her a mysterious aura. She also had a slight accent that made her seem otherworldly, almost European. I admired her self possession from afar as she seemed older, more assured of herself than the rest of us wondering what we would do with ourselves after graduation. True to form, Sonya did not fill out the questionnaire published by the party committee, nor did she stand and repeat her history since graduation. I wish I'd realized it wasn't a requirement for a happy life.

I had little interaction with her until one day when Jill, the class Beatle fan who often spoke in her version of an Iowan Liverpudlian accent complete with slang, cornered me. Sonya was angry because I had told the school principal she smoked. I think that's what Jill meant. "Oy, bird, Sonya is really cheesed off, you chewed the fat and ratted on her and the fags she smokes to our ole govner."

Our "ole govner" was a kindly but strict principal by the name of Mr. Shepherd, but he allowed us to

47

call him Shep. The school board consisted of seven local businessmen who were routinely reelected because no one ran against them. We would hear pronouncements from them read by Shep at school assemblies. "The school board has decided to purchase a scoreboard for the football field." "The school board has decided to resurface the floor of the basketball court." In all fairness, there was probably also an announcement, "The school board has decided to buy more books for the library."

One of my fellow graduates at the reunion was now the president of the school board. "Keep your test covered up," Mr. Hacker, the basketball coach, drivers' ed instructor and part-time history teacher, would say to me. "Johnson is trying to copy off you." I never received an answer for why he didn't just get on Johnson's case. As school board president was Johnson finally being rewarded or punished for his dishonesty? Hacker, of course, was at the reunion. Some people you can only stop by driving a stake through the heart. He delighted in calling me once again by my maiden name. I responded with the truth, "It's been a long time since anyone's called me by that name." The party planners were delighted to have him tell the tale of how he'd dressed up in a cheerleader's uniform to inspire the team to beat our great rival a few towns over. Then they supplied him with a radio remote toy car so he could once again demonstrate how to parallel park a car. "He always got too close to me in that driver's ed car," my friend Harriet whispered to me as he systematically mowed down miniature orange cones for old times' sake.

The superintendent of the school district showed up once a year to sit with us at the lunch table and eat our creamed beef, creamed potatoes, creamed corn, a "dream" cookie and a pint of milk. Our day-to-day discourse was with Shep and his wife, Julia, who was his secretary. If you married a school administrator, you automatically became a school secretary. Now in their mid-eighties they both attended the reunion as it seems they always did. This one was particularly sad as their daughter, a member of my graduating class, had been recently killed in an automobile accident.

Why would Sonya think I told Shep she smoked? I didn't know she smoked. I didn't know anyone smoked. I thought smoking was an adult thing you did like drink coffee or having sex. Young people weren't supposed to do any of those things. The only smokers were the "bad boys" as it went with their cultivated image of leather jackets and terrorizing the younger kids on the school bus. I never actually saw them smoke; I just heard about it.

What to do about Sonya? I couldn't bring it up at home. My father would say, "Ask your mother," and my mother would say, "Just smile and go about your business." Once again, I realized my family was not like those on television. Lassie and Timmy's parents would have given some useful advice.

I got tired of worrying about it and decided to approach her. The confrontation took place in that bastion of high school drama, the girls' restroom. "Sonya, I never told Shep you smoked. I don't care if you smoke." Her answer was simple, "I don't. My boyfriend does. My mom and dad don't like him. I told some people I smoked so it would get back to my parents. They could smell smoke on me and not think I'd been with him. I really hoped you had told Shep." Forty years later it was still silly, and we laughed about it. When I asked about the smoky boyfriend, she didn't answer. She just gave me her best Mona Lisa look.

We all keep secrets. The biggest secrets are those that families keep from each other, from those we should trust the most. Parents and children both practice the "wicked web" of deception. As the youngest, I would hear from my parents, "Don't tell your sisters." From my sisters, I would hear, "Don't tell Mom and Dad." Despite surviving the Depression and World War II or maybe because of it, my oldest sister was quite the style maven. All of her life she liked pricey things, like designer bags, alligator shoes, and new cars. As a young lady my parents bought her a new dress in 1944 to wear while she danced with the servicemen at the local USO. That's how she won World War II. It cost a whopping $5.00, which, according to the story, was a lot of money then. Still, my mother said, "Edith won't wear that. It didn't cost enough money." My father, who seemed to have had much practice in what women wanted, put a one in front of the five on the price tag. It was easy to do in a world without electronic tags. She went to her grave never knowing the real price of her dress.

My sister Janyce had a much better "don't tell" story. Janyce fit the pattern for the rebellious middle child. In that universal triangle of two sisters gossiping about the third, Edith had told me how Janyce was opening defiant: not helping with chores, drinking soda pop and eating candy instead of sitting at the table for supper. I couldn't imagine getting away with such crimes. Having read too many Cherry Ames Student Nurse books, she decided she wanted to be a nurse. My father drove her the fifty miles to Omaha and enrolled her in nursing school. I think she beat him home. She literally tied the bed sheets together in her dorm room and escaped out the window and hitchhiked back to the farm. Years later I had to ask her about it. "Don't tell Mom, but one day in that place was enough. All those girls did was talk

about how the rubbers broke when they had sex. I
didn't want to be a nurse anyway."

I never did anything scandalous enough to beg my
sisters "not to tell." When I was growing up, I didn't
really remember them until they were leading lives of
their own. My oldest sister, Edith, was married with
my nephew three months younger than I was and my
niece two years younger. Janyce was married and
working for an insurance company.

Most of my life I heard from my mother how ex-
hausting I was. It had been sixteen years since she'd
had a baby. She thought that was all over. I was a
surprise. I was a mistake. She was too old and too
tired to have another baby. Accordingly Janyce, who
was sixteen when I was born, took care of me. Janyce
chose my name. I have baby pictures of Janyce holding me but no pictures of me with my parents until I
was four or five. When I was a senior in high school,
Janyce had a baby girl, Theresa. She already had a
three-year-old son, Aaron. I loved being with both of
them, but Mom wouldn't allow me to be seen in public
alone with them in case someone would think they
were my "baby brother or sister" birthed in another
county. I imagine that my mother had the same irra-
tional fears when Janyce was lugging me around, but
my father had just died and I didn't want to distress
Mom further by pointing out her foolishness.

After the reunion and my conversation with Sonya
about why I write biographies, I began to think of myself as a topic. There was so much I didn't know. So
many secrets I suspected but had never confronted.
As a biographer I start with a timeline on my subject, and I make connections. I was born in 1949. My
mother was born in February 1911. She would have
just turned 38 when I was born. Thirty-eight is not
so old to have a baby today, but after World War II

maybe thirty-eight was the present fifty-eight. Janyce was sixteen years older. My mother would have been twenty-two when she was born. I have often felt sorry for my mother with a rebellious teenager and a new baby and a husband always working even if he was just a few feet from the house. Edith was twenty-four years older than I was. My mother would have been fifteen when she was born. No matter how I did the math, my mother would have gotten pregnant at fourteen! My father would have been nineteen when he knocked her up.

My dad, the old dog. My mom, hot to trot. They actually had raging hormones. There was more going on at those dances than just dancing. It explained much, but then again, absolutely nothing. If you started having children at fourteen, by thirty-eight you would feel too old to have another one especially if you were also a full-time farm hand as well as wife and mother. Was this why I got such mixed messages on boyfriends and being a good girl? Is this why she attached such scandal to someone who "had to get married"? Had my grandfather put the symbolic shotgun to my father's back? Did this explain the tension between my mother and my father's mother? Did all of this explain why Mom told me to "go play" when I wanted details of my sisters' weddings? When I asked my sisters about their weddings, they both said they had come home, announced they were getting married, and that was that. They were both married by justices of the peace. As a 14 year old, I wanted to hear tales of frilly white dresses, a dozen bridesmaids, leaving the church in a horse drawn carriage like Cinderella. At least I had a church wedding, a white dress, a reception with a cake and my sisters were there. My parents never attended any of their daughters' weddings.

I never heard my sisters or aunts talk about what my calculations had revealed to me. They must have known. My Aunt Ethel, one of Mom's five living sisters, once brought the family Bible with her on a visit. It was the size of a concrete block, and I couldn't wait to get my hands on it. The Bible contained photos, notes on bits of paper, pages of family members begetting. My Aunt Ethel showed me swatches of her sisters' wedding dresses preserved in the Bible. None were white. They were striped or polka dots or solid colors. "Here is Aunt Nellie's, Aunt Laura's, Aunt...." Of course I asked, "But where's...." Before I even got the question out of my mouth, the Bible was closed. My mother picked it up and carried it out of the room. That was the first and last time I saw that family history. I don't know what happened to it. As a researcher rejoicing in minutiae about others, I have mourned its loss all of my life.

I don't know what my mother's dreams were as a fourteen year old, but she must have had them. Whatever her dreams might have been, she must have known she couldn't achieve them with a baby on the way and a new husband not much older than she was. Maybe her lifelong secrecy kept the loss of those dreams as hidden as that family Bible.

*Your author, her paternal grandmother, and her sister Janyce*

# FARM LIFE IS TOLERANCE

D iscussed at the reunion, when we weren't re-
living our pasts, was that a district court was
soon to rule on the legality of same-sex marriages.
An Iowa court judge had ruled a state law limiting
marriage to a man and woman as a violation of con-
stitutional rights. By 2009 the Iowa Supreme Court
upheld the judge's decision, making Iowa the third
state in the nation to recognize same-sex marriages.
I wasn't surprised. Iowans have always had a live-
and-let-live attitude.

Another popular topic was the upcoming Iowa caucus in January, election year 2008. Iowans take pride in
being the first litmus test for presidential candidates.
Barrack Obama won his party's support in the Iowa
caucus, and we all know what happened after that. As
his mother was from Kansas, he was our neighbor.

My graduating class was diverse in how it reflected
the Irish, Scots, German, Polish, Scandinavian, English and other northern Europeans who had settled
the land generations earlier. Last names varied from
starting with Mc and O' to the Anglo-Saxon "Smith"
and "Jones" to multisyllabic ones that ended in either
"ski" or "son" or "berg" or "stein." My mother's family
was Irish; my father's German. This causes my English husband to shake his head and ask, "How can
you stand yourself?" I think I got the best blend. I'm
organized with a great sense of humor.

The only nonwhites you might see in my farm neighborhood were the original Americans. There was a Sioux Indian reservation just across the Missouri River in Nebraska. Sometimes you would see Indian families in the area grocery stores. The local grocery installed an automatic door, which now is a prerequisite to the title of supermarket, but in the late '50s it was the cutting edge of consumerism. No longer would you have to physically push the door open, just step on the threshold area. Kids, white and native, loved jumping up and down on the doors both opening in and out. All would scurry away when the manager came yelling and running after them. I was in the store with my mother one Saturday while my dad sat in the car and laughed at the kids opening and closing the doors. When my dad saw us come through the automatic doors, he pulled the cart to the trunk of the car and started loading the groceries. "I don't want to go in that store," my dad said, "If I saw the price of those groceries, I'd run out, and I wouldn't wait for those doors to open. Big chief over there wouldn't wait for the doors to open either. Too much wampum." I heard my mother's sharp intake of breath as she looked at the tall man leaning on the truck next to us. His classic profile looked stern. "Ugh," he said, "white man speak truth. Too much wampum." Then he laughed, "How are you, Lawrence?"

I was always amazed at the number of people my father knew. If I went with him to the sale barn where livestock was bought and sold or the feed store or to an auction, he talked with everyone because they all knew him.

As with so many Indian tribes, the Omaha Indians opened a casino on their land in 1992. During my trip to my high school reunion, I wanted to see the casino. I hear the term "casino," and I think of Vegas with bright lights and Rat Pack imitators and magic shows with exotic animals. The casino of the Omaha Indians was a metal building in a corn-field. From the outside it looked like a machine shed where farmers kept their tractors, plows, mowers, and other large farm equipment. Inside farmers in their overalls played penny slots. The casino closed during the hard economic times of 2009. Even gambling couldn't secure the tribe revenge for General Custer or John Wayne.

As an educator, I saw the emphasis on more diversity, multiculturalism in our classrooms: more readings from women, different sexual orientations, and other races than just dead old white men. I grew up in an atmosphere of prejudice against only one group of people—those deemed not working hard enough. You might be poor, but that didn't mean you couldn't work toward making your lot in life better.

My father didn't understand our neighbors, the Wadsworths. Actually, he felt sorry for the wife and two little girls; it was Sam he didn't like. Sam was lazy. "He's got 400 acres of good river bottom land. He should be planting soy beans and corn." If Sam got half of the acreage planted, my dad took it as a good sign that things were turning around. He kept no live-stock, which was probably good as he never repaired fences. The house and outbuildings went unpainted year after year. When his mailbox keeled over from neglect, he left it there causing our mailman, Ernie, to get out of his car and put the mail in the mailbox on the ground. It was a nice thing for Ernie to do, but it probably broke all kinds of federal laws. My father and other neighbors offered to help, to plow or loan equipment, but Sam refused. I'm not sure what his problem was. At that time it would have been nearly impossible to get alcohol in Iowa. I don't think he had the energy to drive across the river into Nebraska so I don't think he drank. Marijuana grew wild, but farmers sprayed it as a weed not knowing you could smoke it unless informed by a friend or relative from the big city. Whatever the reason, it was obvious that Sam Wadsworth didn't want to be a farmer.

Finally, things became unbearable for Mrs. Sam. She left. No farm wife left her husband; no farm wife got a divorce. Worst of all, she left her two little girls. I was on the school bus as usual the morning after everyone knew about Mrs. Sam. As the bus approached the two little girls standing at the downed mailbox in front of their house, Titch looked up in the rearview mirror at his passengers and shouted, "I don't want to hear a word out of anyone!" It was one of the kindest acts I've ever witnessed. Eventually, the farm and what little equipment Wadsworth had went under the auctioneer's gavel. The three of them left the area to places unknown. One of the saddest occasions for a farm community is the dispersal of a neighbor's property, seeing possessions that you associate with a certain family going to others. It often accompanies a death. A year later I would see the new owner of my father's Chevy pickup drive it south away from our farm.

My father had been given a diversity education by being poor. He was born in 1906 and raised in northeastern Kansas. According to my mother, Dad's father might have been rich if it wasn't for his wife, the only living grandparent I barely knew as she died when I was eight. They would homestead and farm an area. When they nearly owned the property, my grandmother would want to move. With six boys and two girls, maybe they always needed more room. Eventually they ended up in western Iowa.

Dad used to tell me about his best friend, Benjy. Benjy's parents had gone to the big city to work, so Benjy was being raised by his grandparents, who were old with white hair. They had been slaves. That connection made the Civil War not so far in the past. I can still surprise friends and family by finishing a gospel song when I've only heard the first few words of it. "How do you know that song?" My dad attended church with Benjy and his grandparents and could sing "sorrow songs" with the best of them. On the other side of the coin, Dad also listened to the Friday and Saturday night jam sessions of blues and jazz sitting outside the local juke joint with Benjy. They were too young to be allowed inside. Sometimes the revelers brought them soda pop.

Although no one in my family can play a musical instrument more complicated than a radio, we had a good foundation in the classics of American music because of Dad. For my older sisters he made comparisons to the Big Band sound or Elvis with what he'd heard as a boy in Kansas. When I played my Rolling Stones albums in the early '60s, his response to Keith Richards was, "He really flew into that guitar. He sounds like Benjy's cousin Crossroads Slim."

I could always tell when we were about to have company, which wasn't often. My sisters with husbands and children came home several times a year usually in the summer and around the holidays. We might have aunts and uncles over for Sunday dinner. When my mother started cleaning as if President Kennedy and Jackie were on their way, it meant we would have guests that we didn't often see such as our landlady. "Who's visiting, Mom?"

"Your dad's old friend, Benjy, and his wife Maryann."

I welcomed the idea of seeing anyone who wasn't my parents, my neighbors, or the kids and teachers at school I saw every day. I was excited—someone from Dad's past and the grandson of a slave. Before I could say anything, my mother laid down the rules, "Don't you dare stare at them because they are Negroes."

My dad chimed in, "They prefer Black. I've heard Benjy and his cousins call each other nigger, but they don't like whites calling them that." Afro-American and African American would come later.

"Well, they call them Negroes on the news," retorted my mother.

Black, Negro, whatever, they were all over the news. The early '60s was the time of Civil Rights, of sit-ins at segregated lunch counters, fire hoses and dogs turned on demonstrators, the death of Medgar Evers and Martin Luther King Jr.'s "I Have a Dream" speech at the Lincoln Memorial. Despite what was going on around the country, there were no blacks in our area. They lived in Sioux City or Omaha. Until I went to college, what I knew of their lives was what I saw on television, what I'd heard from my father or from Benjy and Maryann.

As a child I was a voracious reader. At some point I started studying slavery and the Civil War. The more I read, the more I learned that people down through history seemed all too ready to sell their fellow human beings into bondage. This horrified me. I remember approaching my mother in disgust, "Do you know that people actually bought and sold other people?" I must have sounded accusatory, for her reply was, "Well, I didn't do it." Then came her ultimate dismissal, "Now, go play."

Benjy and Maryann arrived on a Saturday afternoon. Like Cora Jane they rolled down the driveway in their Cadillac. Benjy was tall and lanky and my father was short and round unlike his tall blond, blue-eyed Hitler youth-looking brothers. Benjy grabbed and hugged him all the time laughing and shouting. "Lawrence, you old devil, you." I'd never seen my father hugging anyone or being hugged or being called a devil. My mother and Maryann were polite and reserved toward each other just like spouses of friends. Benjy and Maryann shook my hand. "So this is the baby. How's your two other girls?" Benjy's son was now in the Army.

They ate supper with us. It was our usual summer meal of fried chicken and corn on the cob. These are delicacies to me today, but at twelve years of age I was pretty sick of it. My parents as survivors of the Depression vowed like Scarlett O'Hara that they would never be hungry again. Summer was for any vegetables in the garden, and we had a lot of corn and spare chickens. We saved the pork and beef in our two freezers for the winter months. What we didn't eat out of the garden in the summer, my mother canned and stored in the root cellar. Their "waste not wants not" example stayed with me.

Although my husband's parents had hard times during and following World War II when food was scarce in Britain, he will deem a ketchup bottle empty while I will add vinegar to stretch it a few more meals. He's even been known to feed the heels, the first and last slices of bread, to the birds.

According to the family and the area, my mother was a "helluva" cook and baker of bread, pies, cakes, cookies. For dessert we had chocolate pie. It was all from scratch: the crust, the filling, the meringue topping. When she set it on the table, my dad and Benjy burst into laughter. When Benjy laughed, he did it with his whole body, flashing his white teeth, and clapping his hands. It made you want to laugh, too, even if you didn't know what was so funny. My mother and Maryann looked puzzled. My dad explained, "When we were kids, the local druggist said he would give us five cents if we collected rags for him. I don't know what he used them for, but a nickel was a lot of money then. We went door to door taking any rags people could spare."

Benjy took up the story. "We did; we did. Worked all day to get those rags. We got ourselves that nickel, and we bought ourselves a chocolate pie. My grandpa picked us up in his horse and wagon. Lawrence put the pie on the back of the wagon. When I got in the wagon, I put my foot in the pie." They howled in laughter. "Yeah, yeah, Lawrence said he couldn't tell if my foot was in the pie 'cause my foot was as dark as the chocolate."

"Did you eat the pie?" I asked.

"You bet," my dad said. "A nickel was too hard to come by."

After supper the old friends sat outside and talked, while I helped the women folk in the traditional clearing of the table and doing the dishes. Mom and Maryanne talked of recipes and children. Maryanne told us how she worked in a hotel cleaning rooms while Benjy worked for the railroad. "I just gotta be a housewife and a maid," Maryanne said to my mother. "You gotta be a wife and a farm hand. You do women's work and men's work." My mother issued one of her usual platitudes of acceptance, "I get by."

After I went to bed, I could still hear them talking and laughing. Benjy brought out what my dad called a "blues harp" and started to play. I could hear feet stamping and hands clapping to the music. At some point they switched to gospel. I fell asleep to "Rock my soul in the bosom of Abraham. Oh, Lord, rocka my soul."

The next morning our company was gone. I helped my mother change the sheets on the bed where Benjy and his wife had slept. When I picked a pillow up, there lay a shiny nickel.

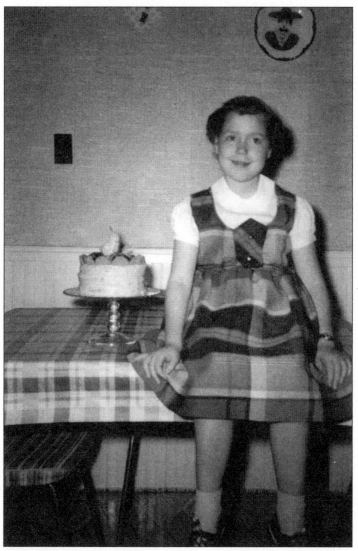

*Your author with an infamous bad perm at Easter with one of my mother's legendary cakes*

# FARM LIFE IS A FEMINIST MOVEMENT

W hen I left high school there were rumblings of another feminist movement. Every hundred years or so, women get tired of taking care of others and make some demands. I think few of my "sisters" in my class doubted we would be wives and mothers, but we also wanted more. Forty years had made a difference. At the reunion I surmised we all had worked outside the home at some point in our lives. Many of us had specialized training and careers in education, medicine, and the business world. We'd had good examples to follow. Of the sixteen teachers at the high school level, six were women. They weren't all in home economics. I had women teachers in math, business, literature, languages, and science. If they made as much money as their male counterparts, I don't know, but I bet they didn't.

My mother also worked "outside the home" in the fields. That's what farmers' wives did. My aunts on both my mother's and father's side of the family drove tractors and fed livestock as well as kept house and raised children. Only my Uncle John, one of my father's older brothers, married a "city woman." I remember my Aunt Florence as a rather nervous woman who was always in a nice dress, jewelry, nylons, and high heels. My mother only dressed up for church or such rituals as a wedding or a funeral.

I don't know where my Uncle John met my Aunt Florence. In the city, I guess, but everyone knew she wasn't much help at his place, and she wasn't a cook either. If we ate Sunday dinner with them, we politely ignored the lack of gravy, which my mother took as a sacred complement for any meat. If she put a charred meatloaf on the table, Uncle John would grin and say, "Florence needs to learn that you can't cook everything on high." He never said anything like that in her presence, so he must have loved her. I enjoyed talking with her. When she asked to see my eighth grade class picture, she successfully picked out the boy I had a crush on. This proves culinary skills can be overrated. My mother and my other aunts seemed to like her just fine. Perhaps they envied her only job of keeping house.

On February 3, 1962 the world was supposed to end—again. Pluto was still a planet, and eight of the nine planets were aligning like a cosmic shish ka bob. That seemed as good a reason as any for the world to end. Druids were dancing around Stonehenge, Eskimos were chanting, churches were holding prayer sessions. It was pretty scary for a thirteen year old. My father dismissed it all as foolishness. He watched the people gyrating on television and declared, "You can't do nothing with people who want to sing and dance all the time." It was not only his entire foreign policy, but also his philosophy of life. When your work was done, then you could sing and dance but not before.

Some seer had set the end to begin at 2:00 p.m. Central Time. It was Saturday, and I was at a 4-H meeting at our house. Our group, the Farmerettes, rotated the monthly meetings among the homes of the members. In those days 4-H was separated by sex. The boys showed livestock and grains at fairs while the girls showed their cooking, sewing, and decorating skills. I did well as a cook and seamstress as I'd had a talented guru in my mother to teach me these arts. When the world didn't end, I even got a blue ribbon at the Iowa State Fair for a butter cake I made. It had taken weeks of making yellow cakes after yellow cakes and freezing the best to be transported to Des Moines. I still won't eat yellow cake. I got so sick of creaming butter and sugar by hand with a big wooden spoon that my dad would take over the task while I rested my hands and arms. All of that smashing together of fat and sweet was necessary to make a light, fluffy cake. Maybe you can use a food processor today, but it hadn't even been invented when I dedicated myself to Head, Heart, Hands, and Health. I still fear the Iowa State Fair police will show up at my door one day and demand my blue ribbon back for violating some rule about family members helping you make your cake.

My Aunt Ethel, my mother's sister with the forbidden family Bible, was certain I would take my yellow cake on to the World's Fair in Seattle, which had opened in April 1962. My mother and I kept trying to tell her, "It's not that type of fair." It showcased technical advancements not the skills of junior Iowa bakers. "They have a monorail and a space needle." We would think we had her convinced and then she would ask, "When are you going to start baking for the World's Fair?" My father always knew that while a loving woman, Aunt Ethel inhabited her own little world. After all, she had married a man who raised and showed horses. For Dad that was a hobby not a legitimate farm living. I eventually got Aunt Ethel off the World's Fair cake topic by telling her that I hadn't placed. Now I would also be in the crosshairs of World's Fair police for lying.

Our 4-H meeting was supposed to center on learning how to make a mat to frame a photo. No one could concentrate. We watched the clock and talked about the world ending. My friend Linda said, "Cows are sacred in India, and the Indians are making butter from the cream of these cows. When they get the butter churned, the world will end." It sounded as plausible as any other observation.

Close to the appointed time, 2:00 pm, someone knocked on our door. Was it the angel Gabriel about to blow his horn? We could hear voices—my mother's and I recognized my Uncle John. When my mother came back to our living room, she informed our group leader, "I have to leave for awhile. I won't be long." As I looked out of our living room window, I saw my mother and my Uncle John leaving in his truck. My dad stood in the driveway.

How could my mother leave if the world was about to end? My father didn't seem too concerned. Somehow we survived the 2:00 end time. In another hour we displayed our matted photos in cheap frames and had our snack. By 4 o'clock, all of the Farmerettes had been picked up by their mothers. It was then my dad said, "We have to go get your mother."

"What happened, Dad?"

"Your Aunt Florence got scared about the world ending. She climbed up in a tree and wouldn't come down. That's why your Uncle John came to get your mother." My unflappable, rational mother had talked down my aunt sitting in a tree with a packed suitcase waiting for Jesus or churned butter.

When we got to my uncle's home, Aunt Florence was drinking tea. Her hair was askew, her nylons ripped, her dress dirty. Her suitcase was at the side of the couch. It was obvious that she had been crying. I knew better than to say anything. We rode home in silence, me sitting between my parents. Over the weeks that followed, I would listen for snippets of conversation between my parents. Poor Florence, she tried, she never fit in, she was too nervous, poor Uncle John. Their tone changed over time when it was discovered that Aunt Florence was sick. She had a brain tumor. She was in and out of the hospital for a while, and we went to see her when she was sent home because her world was about to end. She was very ill with a big ribbon on her head where her thick black hair had once been. She was lying on the couch in a nice dress, nylons and lots of bangley jewelry. She jangled as she held my arm. "Goodbye, Reese Ann. You be as strong as your mother, and you'll do good."

My mother was not only emotionally strong, but she was also physically strong from all the toting and lifting she did. Madonna's or Michelle Obama's arms had nothing on my mother's. Carrying buckets of feed or milk, pitching hay, pushing a cow or hog into a barn was a better workout than any personal trainer could imagine. When I asked to see her muscles, she always gave me the sideways World War II Rosie the Riveter poster "We can do it!" bended arm with the bulging bicep. She also had strong legs, and she was fast. I once saw her clear a four foot fence on a run because she was being chased by a sow with a new litter of baby pigs. I'm sure adrenaline contributed to the speed and height of her Olympic form.

My mother was nine years old when the 19th Amendment to the Constitution was ratified in 1920 and women could vote. She voted for the first time in 1932 for Franklin Roosevelt. My parents discussed politics, and both took voting very seriously. My father evoked images of fallen patriots. While he was always a Roosevelt Democrat because he believed we wouldn't have survived the Depression or won World

War II without "Roosy," he prided himself on not voting strictly by party. "I'll vote for any man who'll do me some good." Did my parents ever consider the remote possibility of electing women? Yet, it's my mother's words that get me out to even the smallest election; "Women were ridiculed, jailed, forcefed because they demanded the vote. It's the duty of every woman to vote because of their sacrifice."

Traditional farms of fifty years ago without the advanced automation of today needed big families, preferably of boys. Once you could walk and talk, you could do the simplest of chores: pull weeds in the garden, pick up nuts in the fall, scatter corn for chickens. As you grew older and stronger your chores increased in complexity and strength. Once you began driving a tractor there was so much more you could do: plant, harvest, haul something to another field. Boys were preferred simply because they were stronger. I watched my neighbor's sons pick up fifty pound bales of hay, one in each hand, and throw them on a truck. They could wrestle a cow or pig to the ground to be vaccinated. I could carry about four kittens in my hands.

I did my part because I felt some residual guilt for not being male or for being a surprise or a burden to my mother. Mainly, I helped by doing some of her farm jobs. If I did her chores during the busiest times of planting and harvesting, I freed her up for the role of "hired hand," so she could help out my dad. I gathered and washed eggs. At any time we had around a hundred hens. When they were laying eggs, they were laying eggs! Although we had a special coop where the eggs rolled down to a protected shelf, they still got dirty because of where they left the hen. I gathered the eggs and washed them. They could be nasty. I didn't hear a lot of swearing, but occasionally my father or one of my uncles would call someone a "chicken shit." I understood perfectly what a dastardly guy you had to be to earn that epithet.

After washing the eggs and letting them dry, I put them into cartons that held twelve layers of twelve eggs each to be picked up once a week by the egg buyer for a hefty fifty cents a dozen. Sometimes our neighbors who didn't have chickens or whose hens had stopped laying bought eggs from us. Farm families needed lots of eggs because it took lots of cooking and baking to keep those big families of boys working.

We also had a dozen or so cows. When they calved, they had to be milked. Our farm wasn't a dairy so we had no automatic milking machines. At any time we probably only milked around four cows. We sold the milk to the same farmers' cooperative that bought our eggs, and we kept some for our own use. With a Ph.D. in English, you have few physical skills beyond typing, so I'm proud to say I can still milk a cow. It is just like riding a bicycle or swimming, you never forget how to do it. If you got good at the squeezing and aiming into a bucket, you could shoot a stream of milk into a cat's mouth at ten foot. I tell my cats about this as they stand at the refrigerator that supplies their milk. Unimpressed, they swish their tales and demand cream.

Mom needed our eggs and milk for her own kitchen. I helped my mother cook and bake for the harvesting crews in the fall. Families in our neighborhood banded together to get in everyone's crops. Neighbors came and helped you, and you went and lent them a hand. During these times, the cooking crew of women neighbors also circulated from farm to farm racing the weather. It was an intense couple of weeks of dawn to dark and sometimes after dark for farmers to get their crops harvested and stored before the fall rains started. After the rain, frost on the pumpkin would follow quickly.

It began with breakfast at first light. Eight to ten husbands, fathers, sons would eat a huge breakfast of eggs, bacon, bread, fried potatoes and coffee while another ten or so would be gassing up tractors or preparing combines. The first group would go out and head to the fields and the second wave would come to breakfast. They ate and went into the fields. By then it was midmorning and the first breakfast eaters were ready for a snack—coffee, cookies, cake or pie. Then it was time for the next crew's coffee break. Then it was lunchtime, afternoon snack, supper. Sometimes after supper the crews returned to the fields to work with lights on their combines and trucks. The next day it started all over again. This was how they brought in the corn, soy beans, wheat, and sorghum.

You would get the dishes done for one group and another would come in ready to eat. The dozen or so women enjoyed the busy camaraderie. They would say things like "They sure can put it away!" "It's good to see such healthy appetites." I even got rid of all my yellow cakes.

The meals made and consumed weren't exactly health conscious. Fried chicken, fatty roasts, heavy gravies, vegetables swimming in butter, desserts with whipped or ice cream. I'm still wearing the calories from those meals, but it was worth it. My dad and the other farmers lost weight during harvesting no matter how much they ate. Dad's explanation, "Maybe it makes us thin to carry all the food around inside us." In reality it was probably the pressure of harvest, as most of your yearly income depended upon it, plus the physicality of the work. It was a different type of work for the women, but it was still physical. Because harvesting was as inevitable as fall, my mother prepared for it year round by cooking, baking, and freezing as if on steroids. When she made bread, she made twelve loaves and froze the extras. The same went for casseroles or desserts.

My father once let it slip that he had hoped at the birth of each of his three girls that we would be a boy. All of our neighbors had at least one or more boys to help on the land. Our closest neighbors, the Donaldsons had five, each about a year apart. Accordingly their mother, Ruth, always wanted a girl. Occasionally they would walk the mile to our house and share a meal with us, or we went to their farm north of us "to visit." Ruth doted on me because I was a little girl. She loved my doll house, and she would help me move the furniture about. We colored together or played with paper dolls. She didn't care if I colored outside of the lines or the crayon colors clashed, both unacceptable in our house. When I was older, we looked at dresses and furnishings in catalogs. A story she loved to tell was when my parents and me plus all the Donaldsons were sitting at their dinner table— three women and seven men. I was young, probably somewhere between eight and ten. I piped up, "Ruth, how did you get all these boys?" I'm sure my mother's mouth fell open, but before she could stop me, I looked at the Donaldson patriarch and said, "It's your fault, isn't it?" The kitchen rocked with laughter. I wish I could remember this sitcom scene. Ruth repeated this story as long as we lived south of their farm. I last heard it the day my mother and I moved to town after my father's death.

Because farm life is so testosterone-laden, any female companionship for farm wives is precious. Unlike my mother, Ruth had no female relatives in the area. Mother/son relationships are the substance of comedy and tragedy. My mother didn't like my father's mother. "No one was ever good enough to marry one of her six boys." Not Ruth's philosophy, she welcomed each and every one of her daughters-in-law and all of the grandchildren even if they were boys.

The summer before my father died was not a cheerful one for our farm community. My Uncle John's and Aunt Florence's son who had been in and out of trouble since his mother died went to prison for writing bad checks. The Donaldson's youngest son was drafted and headed to Vietnam. One of the sons of another neighbor ran a stop sign and killed a man who did not know as everyone else in our county did, that the Phelps boys never stopped at that junction. All of this led my father to say to my mother at breakfast one morning, "Maybe it's just as well we had girls."

*Your author in the graduation portrait compromise hairdo*

*Proof #8*

# FARM LIFE IS LAUGHTER

S ince I sat down and filled out the questionnaire for the reunion, I am still trying to think of something funny that happened during my high school years. "What is your funniest memory from high school? THINK. We all have them if we can remember back that far or are honest/brave enough to share." Twelve exclamation points followed "share." One of my coping skills I learned on the farm when things got grim was to ask myself: What's funny about this?

I found the whole reunion funny, in laughter and oddity, because of the glory wallowing some were doing. Others found humor in class incidents or nicknames of particular teachers. One coach won his handle Magilla after a cartoon character because he had a rolling gorilla gait as he walked. One of the class "hoods" confessed to putting an outhouse outside the high school one Halloween. Another remembered stacking up burnt grilled cheese sandwiches in a lunchtime protest and being sent to the principal's office.

Just hearing my friend Karen laugh made me laugh even if I had no idea what she found so funny. Karen, Joey and I had started public school education together and graduated together. Joey's comment on Karen's giggling was, "She'd laugh if you ran over her foot with a lawn mower." I was sitting with her on the bus one morning when the Schultz kids got on the bus, two boys and two girls. The oldest girl was our classmate, Cheryl. Karen burst into laughter, and as usual, I joined her as did many others, which earned us dagger glances from Titch. When we quieted down, I asked as usual, "What's so funny?" "Giggle, giggle, snort, snort. I was just thinking how much time it must take Cheryl to do her hair every morning. Ha ha ha hee hee."

This was an era when girls either ironed, with real ironing board irons, their hair so it would be straight or spent half their lives in pink, spongy hair rollers to get that smooth under curl or upwards flip. They even slept in them. Some went so far as to roll up their hair in metal orange juice or lemonade juice cans to get that big, bouncy look. Poor Cheryl's hair had looked the same since kindergarten. It had obviously never seen the inside of what was known then as a beauty parlor. I was fortunate, considering my yearly curly perm, to have a cousin who had her parlor in her home, as was the way before strip malls. Cheryl's family couldn't afford such luxuries. Her bangs were cut straight across, as was the rest of her haircut just below her ears. At least she didn't have the bowl-on-the-head, Norman knight look of the Middle Ages sported by her two brothers. It was funny to think of her sleeping in rollers every night to always have the same non-effect. Fortunately, no one took offense at Karen's laughter, as we were never certain what tickled her funny bone. I wish she had attended the reunion; I know I would have laughed until I cried. I had to settle for her response to the question on remembering something funny: "Too many to write here."

Every few months the high school students would be herded into the gym for an assembly. Sometimes our band or instrumental groups would play, and some of my courageous fellow students would sing or dance. It might be a professional entertainer like a magician making balloon animals or a lecturer who talked to us about the evils of sex or alcohol. A county health official once admonished the girls in the audience to always carry a phone book with them in case they found themselves in a crowded car and had to sit on the lap of a boy. What bravery of those people to travel around in their cars and perform before several hundred high schoolers who scoffed at anything and everything. I remember one lady who couldn't sing a lick. She would disappear behind a screen, make a brief wardrobe change and come out and sing a song appropriate to her outfit. As a gypsy woman with a scarf on her head and a tambourine, she ducked behind the screen to return with a sombrero and a guitar singing "La Cucaracha." We laughed as our teachers all scowled at us and poked at students closest to them. Truth be known, they were as happy to be out of class as we were, yet they realized what I now do. Miss Rosarita was just trying to make a buck. Once she might have dreamed of Broadway or the movies. She would have rejoiced at Branson, Missouri if it had existed then as we know it now. But she didn't give up. She traveled around Iowa from school to school for probably not much money, but she was still in show business.

The nonprofessional talented among the students included lots of accordion players. Because of the German, Polish, Eastern European background of so many farm families, accordion lessons were common. All the Donaldson boys took accordion lessons. Lawrence Welk was from North Dakota, and his picture, complete with accordion, adorned many a community building even in Iowa. Although Welk died in 1992 his spirit lives on in Branson, where he still pulls in plenty of visitors from Iowa and other states north to the Lawrence Welk Resort.

From 1955 on, it was mandatory for my family and our neighbors to watch *The Lawrence Welk Show*. A community who didn't believe in alcohol heard the champagne cork pop, watched the bubbles float upward behind the orchestra, and listened to the champagne lady sing. A friend's mother had actually danced with Lawrence Welk. At the end of his show, Welk would pluck ladies from the audience to dance with him. Mrs. Vonhagen even had an autographed photo on her living room wall to prove it. She was the biggest celebrity in our area only to be surpassed in a few years by a local Miss America contestant. Judy Haley Morris had graduated a few years ahead of me and attended a university north of our area. Blonde, smiling, she had been a cheerleader, a baton twirler, a homecoming queen, and a regular assembly singer. That must have been why she was bitten by the pageant bug. She had been Miss Merry Christmas, Miss Fourth of July, Miss County Fair. Now she was Miss Northern State and would be going to Atlantic City. Our farming community was all abuzz. Whether you were in the grocery store, at the doctor's, getting your tires rotated, everyone was talking about Judy becoming Miss America.

As certain as school started in the fall, it was a requirement to watch the Miss America contest. We always watched with the hope that Miss Iowa might win this year. At the very least, we had to cheer her on. This time we actually knew someone from Iowa with a crown and a sash even if she wasn't Miss Iowa. This year the pageant was going to be broadcast in color for the first time.

My father had purchased a Zenith color television that summer when our old black-and-white set refused to be fixed anymore. Televisions consisted of a huge round picture tube for viewing. When you looked in the back of the set you saw a series of smaller tubes where now there are circuit boards. If your TV quit, you didn't throw it out and buy a new one; you fixed it. You might have the TV repairman come to the house or like my father do it yourself. He would take the suspected faulty tubes out of the back console, go to Carlton's store, which was part grocery, appliance and hardware store and test them on the owner's tube tester. If he found one that had no power he bought a replacement, took it home and plugged it into the old tube spot and, voila, most of the time the television worked. When it seemed that my dad and I were always in Carlton's testing tubes, Doug Carlton sensed a possible sale. "Now, Lawrence, you work hard. You deserve a new television. Color TV is not a phase; it is the wave of the future. I'll send this Zenith out to the house, and you can try it. If you don't like it, I'll come pick it up."

"No, that won't be necessary," my dad said. "I'm just having a little trouble with the horizontal. There's a black strip at the bottom of the picture. I think it's all the Westerns we watch. All that dirt from horses and wagons." It made both me and Mr.Carlton laugh, but he honed his sales pitch. "*Bonanza* is in color. It's like Hoss and Little Joe are in the room with you." My father responded with words that I knew meant "yes" in fatherspeak. "We'll see." Truth be known, I think he was enamored of the new technology and the idea of seeing the Ponderosa ranch in "glorious living color" a male voice would intone when the NBC peacock spread its feathers to the sound of harp chords.

Early television was a capricious friend. You were never quite sure what was going to be on or when. We started out with NBC and CBS channels. You could turn the TV on and there would be a test pattern of a profile of an Indian, complete with feathered war bonnet, on top of a circle within a larger circle and framed by four smaller circles. My dad said you were supposed to adjust your television picture with those lines and circles. The only sound you would hear would be a buzzing. In the early days of television you left the set on. If the buzzing stopped or you saw the Indian flicker, it meant something was about to happen. You might get an old movie, the news, or, wonder of wonders, wrestling!

Later on, networks filled out the schedule. *Today* was on early in the morning with host Dave Garroway and his sidekick J. Fred Muggs, a mostly out-of-control chimpanzee, just like talk shows today. Shows for kids followed, *Captain Kangaroo* and *Miss Jane's Schoolroom*. There might be some game shows and soap operas with dramatic organ music in the background to punctuate the moments of high emotion. Fifteen minutes of national news followed by fifteen minutes of local news and weather started the evening. Then came live variety shows and sitcoms. It was all over after *The Tonight Show* first with Steve Allen and later with Jack Parr, years before Johnny Carson and all the wannabes. We also got the PBS channel where we watched plays, operas, documentaries, and Julia Child cook. This was how my dad sold my mother on a new television. We would be able to get educational programs for me. Me, a pawn, in his scheme.

Once delivered, the colored television never went back to Carlton's Store. After over fifty years, it still works. We get it out for "state occasions and royal birthdays" as my husband says and pull out the knob that turns it on. You have to turn the round knob (clunk clunk clunk) to find a channel. The picture is hazy, the sound low, but it can place me back in my parents' living room with the neighbors who just happened to "stop by" to see the brave new world of television in color.

Our house was packed the night of the Miss America show. In an attempt to prolong her fifteen minutes of Lawrence Welk fame, Mrs. Vanhagen regaled us with details of Judy Haley's reign. As Judy Haley's second grade teacher, she had insider information. "Do you know she can't wear shorts when she drives around in the car that has the 'Miss Northern State' decal on the side? No, no, she has to be fully dressed with her tiara on her head."

"I saw her and waved at her," said our hired hand Robert. "I didn't see no terrier." Robert had a terrier named Nipper. The image of Judy with a small dog on her head made me laugh. Robert was oblivious but laughed with everyone anyway.

Robert lived in an old trailer by the river with Nipper. Today we would say he was "challenged," but he was a hard worker. My dad hired Robert on a day-to-day basis, meals included, when he needed extra help. Robert followed instructions to the exact word, so my dad had to say, "When you see me stop the combine, drive the truck under the spout and I'll load the truck. Then you stay there until I stop again." As one of Robert's limited sources of income, my dad tried to keep him as busy as possible. Winter could be lean times or as my dad said, "All the money goes out in the cold." Yet, he found things for Robert to do. I remember Robert spending a day sorting out my dad's nuts and bolts into nice neat rows on top of Dad's workbench.

Robert was dependable. Summertime in Iowa meant storms often tornadoes. On a hot, quiet day we saw a series of three tornadoes come down from the black clouds and briefly touch the ground. Our hearts stopped, but then we sighed relief when we saw each of the twisters ascend back into the sky. Down the driveway came Robert and Nipper in his old, battered Ford truck. "My God," said my dad. "What are you doing here? Didn't you see those tornadoes?" Robert answered, "I stopped and rolled up my windows." His world was one of terriers as crowns and tornadoes stopped by truck windows.

"Judy Haley's parents must be so proud," said someone.

"Her life is really going to change as Miss America," voiced another.

"Yes, she'll be traveling all over the world representing us."

"What's her talent?"

Mrs. Vanhagen was on that question. "She's doing a medley from *The Sound of Music*. She had to take her musical arrangements and all her costumes with her." Was she going to go behind a screen as a nun and come out as nanny Maria? Had Miss Rosarita entered her psyche? Did I dare disturb the universe and ask the question: What if she doesn't win?

Everyone gathered around the television as the peacock did its thing. "Live from Atlantic City!" Bert Parks greeted the audience there and at home. He introduced the judges, explained the judging system, then the parade of contestants alphabetically by states. "My name is... and I represent the great state of...." The costumes depicting the states, the fixed smiles, the comments in our living room, "She has a nice smile." "That's the best they could find?" "I wish I had a heifer that cute!" Feminist protests of pageants objectifying women would come in a few years, but I never felt sad at the remarks from both men and women in our living room. I did wonder why there was no televised Mr. America contest with swim trunks and tuxedos.

Out of loyalty we cheered for Miss Iowa and cheered louder for Judy Haley in her dirndl top and feminine version of lederhosen. All the contestants lined up. Bert called out the names of the semifinalists who would go on to the next round. The young ladies all continued to smile as there were only a few more states to be pulled out of the crowd. As a name was called, hands went up to a smiling face as the princess progressed forward to stand next to all the other possible queens. The last name was called, and it wasn't Judy Haley Morris of Northern State. The room was still. Mutely, we watched Judy participate in the losers song and dance, a rendition of "Getting to Know You" giving the semifinalists a chance to change wardrobe for the next round of elimination. There would be no *Sound of Music* medley nor would she get to express her desire for world peace.

Robert broke the silence. "I thought she was real pretty. She can borrow Nipper if she needs a terrier."

*The Irish twins, my Aunt Nellie and my mother*

*Proof #9*

# FARM LIFE IS PATRIOTISM

A picture of the president always hung in our living room, no matter the person or the party. The picture, in calendar form, came courtesy of Carlton's Store each year. They gave them out during the Christmas season. I had seen patrons of the store throw down the gift calendar, depending who was on it, with "I won't have that man in my house." The president of not your party was always "that man." "That's rude," my mother would whisper to me. "A gift should be graciously accepted no matter what it is."

As a reader of history, I loved these calendars. The large portrait of the current president would be surrounded by past presidents in clockwise order, with Washington above the twelve at the top of the calendar. Each small portrait of a past president had the years served under his picture. I liked asking people who visited our home who was their favorite president or what year someone was born so I could look up who was president then. My mother quickly judged the birth year question as impolite even if no one threw the calendar on the floor, so I had to limit my curiosity to my family. My father was born under the sign of Theodore Roosevelt, my mother William Taft. My oldest sister came into the world with Calvin Coolidge as president, my other sister under Franklin Roosevelt, 1933. She used to tell me she was born in 1833, which although impossible, would have made her an Andrew Jackson baby. Harry Truman was president when I was born. It was a good mix of Republicans and Democrats.

My parents prided themselves on voting for the person not the party. My father's political philosophy was that all politicians were basically liars and crooks. Democrats taxed and spent too much; Republicans scrimped and spent too much. Despite his beliefs, Dad was a registered Democrat because of Franklin Delano Roosevelt. Ironically, an Iowan, Herbert Hoover was president when the stock market crashed in 1929. He had promised "two chickens in every pot" and a "car in every garage." At least that's what my parents said. Although my parents were in their twenties when the Depression started, it obviously hit them hard. It set their pattern of self-sufficiency by which they lived their whole lives.

I heard Depression stories all my formative years, usually ensconced with expressions of how the younger generation never appreciates what the elder went through. The reward for enduring these harangues is that one day you, too, can rail against some young person, "We were poor. We didn't have iPods. All we had were transistor radios!"

As farmers they couldn't sell crops or livestock, as the prices offered didn't come close to the money and labor in them. So, they truly lived off the land. They burnt the once cash crop of field corn in the house stove for heat or fed it to the livestock. They had milk and eggs. They slaughtered and dressed their own chickens, beef and pork. My mother kept a garden and canned everything and anything. With no or little cash, they bartered with the foodstuffs they now couldn't sell. The Depression stories usually ended with "at least we didn't have to stand in a soup line."

As an adult I realized that most of the food my mother made had origins in the Depression. Things had to be stretched with mayonnaise and hard boiled eggs. We ate lots of "salads"—potato, macaroni, pea, chicken, tuna, salmon, ham. Leftover chicken or beef bones became stock for soups and stews. Eggs and flour were transformed into noodles and dumplings to stretch proteins ever more in casseroles. Lots of milk meant lots of puddings. Graham crackers must have been cheap and plentiful. Pudding pies had graham cracker crusts. One of the first things I learned how to make was a poor person's smore. You mixed cocoa with canned milk to make a chocolate spread to be put between two graham crackers. Unlike Martha Stewart we didn't make our own marshmallows, so that didn't go into the recipe I learned.

For my father, Franklin Roosevelt was a savior. "Without Roosy we would have starved to death." After World War II, Dad added, "Without him we would all be speaking German or Japanese right now." He said this despite his German ancestry. Iowa farmers weren't hyphenated Americans. They were Americans. They loved their country as a place of opportunity and a good life. Maybe that's why they didn't talk much of what brought their ancestors here. I surmised that people were starving in Ireland for my grandfather to leave. From my history studies I knew that posters were hung on trees in Germany enticing people to the New World. Maybe my grandfather, facing compulsory military service, saw one and headed west. If my parents knew, they never said. My questions got the response, "That was so long ago." They concentrated on the now.

As a writer, I'm often asked to speak to various social clubs who revere their ancestors and how long they've been in America. It is amusing to me they limit membership to those descended from *signers* of the Declaration of Independence or someone who swabbed the deck of the Nina, the Pinta or Santa Maria. Exclude me if you like, but I can trace my Methodist ancestry back to Adam and Eve.

A prisoner of war camp existed from 1943-1946 not far from our farm. There were a number of camps housing Axis prisoners throughout Iowa. As the middle of the country, it would have been difficult for Hitler, Mussolini or Tojo to attempt any type of rescue. One might question the wisdom of putting mostly German prisoners in an area with people who could have been related to them. My two sisters, who were seventeen and ten, would walk over to the encampment and wave at the young men. Years later they told me, "They mostly looked like our uncles, but some were cute." My father always said of those prisoners, "They didn't have any choice. They were just doing their jobs." In England my husband's aunt once told me of how her mother, my husband's paternal grandmother, had cornered a parachuted German with her pitchfork. "He was scared and except for his language and uniform, he looked like one of us. He was just doing his job."

Several in my graduating class had been in the military, had made careers in it and had even been to Vietnam. Two died there. At that time young males had to register for the mandatory draft. I had to explain to my students the draft lottery system instituted in 1969 when the birth date of young males determined the order they would be going into the Army if they didn't volunteer for a branch of the armed forces first.

Military recruiters would sometimes visit our school to talk to the young men. Women seldom entered the military. I remember a slovenly young lady from the graduating class ahead of me. She usually looked like she'd been pulled through a knothole backwards as we used to say. She sat at the back of the class and when called upon stared at her desk and mumbled. Not surprisingly, Betty couldn't find a job after graduation and out of desperation joined the Air Force. After her basic training, she came back to school and presented one of those infamous assemblies. The difference was night and day. It made me think that maybe Judy Haley should have joined the Air Force. Where once a slouching, tongue-tied waif in a stained dress stood was now a confident, shoulders back, poised, smiling young woman. Her hair was coifed. She wore foundation and lipstick. Who had the magic wand? She confidently told us about the other young women from all over the country she had met. Her dark blue suit was neatly pressed, and she wore shiny, black dress pumps with, what was the envy of any teenage girl—baby doll heels. The shoes were enough to make me want to sign up. She described the basic training, which sounded much like farm life: rising early, busy all day with physical labor, early to bed. She told us how she'd slept on the floor rather than wrinkle the sheets so her bed would be perfect for inspection. She made a joke about flying a typewriter. Clerical work was as far as most women got in the Air Force in the late '60s. Overall, we were impressed.

When I visited England in the late '60s, looking for a husband or so my husband says, I was aware that World War II seemed as it was yesterday. There were still bombed areas of rubble in London. My host family proudly showed me pictures of the father in the Royal Marines. The young brother of the family innocently asked, "What did your father do in the war?" I answered, "He was a farmer. They wouldn't take him." My host parents said, "They need farmers in war time" when young Paul didn't understand how my father had not been in the war as his dad had been.

When Japan attacked Pearl Harbor, although my father was thirty-five years old, he went to the local recruiters to sign up. He was met with, "Go home, Lawrence. You are too good of a farmer to make a soldier." The sources of this story were my older sisters. My father didn't like to talk about how he had never served his country in the military. When the United States joined World War I, he was around eleven. He taught me how to knit and told me that he had learned as a kid in school because his class knitted socks, gloves and scarves for the troops. He could have up to four needles going as he showed me how to do more intricate stitches needed for sweaters or socks. If I had been knitting for the doughboys, they would have had to be content with uneven squares full of loose stitches.

My parents took two newspapers in addition to the magazines they subscribed to. They also watched the news and any related news programs. It seemed that all television was on Sunday morning was church and politics. The very two things no one is supposed to discuss.

My parents loved elections. The first presidential election I remember was the Kennedy/Nixon election of 1960 when I was eleven. My father watched every minute of both party conventions. Although everyone knew who the party was going to nominate for president, each state had to put forth a home-grown candidate. "The great state of Iowa wishes to nominate that great citizen, great humanitarian, our native son and the next president of the United States... Senator Soybean!" Music, applause, signs hoisted and marching in the aisles. A speech would follow and then on to the next state. It was a political Miss America contest.

I would lie on the couch and whine with boredom until my father said, "Hush, you might learn something." Conventions mattered in those days not the caucuses or the primaries. When you only had two or three television networks and they all covered the conventions "from gavel to gavel" for an entire week per party, you could easily suffer from entertainment deficit syndrome.

My parents wavered back and forth on the pros and cons of John F. Kennedy and Richard Nixon. Nixon had been vice president so he had some experience. He had actually met with our nemesis Nikita Khrushchev of the Soviet Union. Kennedy was a young, charismatic war hero. After eight years of Eisenhower, maybe the country needed a fresh face and party in the White House. I chose Kennedy because Jackie was stylish and seemed happy. Pat Nixon never looked happy to me. Jackie just hid her misery better.

Election night, November 8, 1960, was a real nail biter. We started watching the election returns after the 5:30 p.m. national news. As polls closed, electoral numbers went up slowly because there was no computer counting or projection of winners before people could even mark their paper ballots. My mother and I got tired and went to bed, throughout the night I would get up, go to the living room, and ask Dad, "Is there a winner?" "Not yet," he would reply. I'd go back to bed and get up a few hours later and we'd have the same conversation. Finally, it was 6:20 a.m. Iowa time and NBC declared Kennedy the victor in California, which gave him enough electoral votes to be elected president. The news anchor team of Chet Huntley and David Brinkley turned over the broadcast to *The Today Show* with Dave Garroway. I don't remember if J. Fred Muggs weighed in on the election. If he had perhaps he wouldn't so easily have handed Nixon's home state to Kennedy. When all the votes were counted days later, Nixon had actually won California. It didn't matter. Kennedy still won enough electoral votes of other states to make him president.

I loved that it was such a close contest. I bemoaned elections later when they called winners before everyone got a chance to vote until they ruled that they couldn't call elections until all the polls were closed. I finally got my wish for a close election in 2000 when it took weeks and the Supreme Court to determine who our president was. My dad would have loved it too.

Because of the young vibrant president, his chic first lady and their cute children, I followed their exploits closely. I read books about them and magazine articles. These were all positive stories. Reporting scandal would come later. I didn't know much about Kennedy's plans for the United States, his "New Frontier." I would leave those heavier matters to my parents. Occasionally, I would hear grumblings from fellow students probably repeating what their parents said. "Why is the taxpayer paying to send Jackie and her sister to India?" "You watch, the Russians will test Kennedy."

Growing up I heard much about the "Cold War" between the West and the communist Eastern Bloc and the arms race between the United States and the Soviet Union. Top news stories would be about who had tested atomic weapons above and below ground. It scared me silly. I tried not to think about it. That was difficult as we often heard when you were only fifty miles from Strategic Air Command in Omaha, you would be hit early. Both the president and the Russian leader had these boxes with red buttons always with them. If they accidentally pushed the buttons, it was all over for SAC and for me. In addition to fire drills, we had "duck and cover" drills. A longer version of the fire alarm would go off, and you were expected to get under your desk, butt in the air, your arms covering your head. When I would report to my parents that we had this drill, my dad would chuckle, "Bend over and kiss your sweet ass goodbye!"

Just as Pearl Harbor was a defining day for my parents' generation and 9/11 would be for my students, we all know what happened on November 22, 1963. Like hiding under a desk, it seems so ludicrous now to drive a president in an open car through a crowd and tall buildings. On that Friday afternoon, we were excited about the "big game." There was to be a pep rally in the gym after classes. After lunch Shep came on the intercom to announce that shots had been fired at the motorcade in Dallas. Gasps and shock in English class interrupted our trying to slog through *Silas Marner*. I heard one guy under his breath, "I never liked that man anyway." Minutes later Shep came back on the intercom to announce the president had died. "Good, now Nixon will be president," said the same "that man" detractor. Usually the good girl, I couldn't help myself, "No you idiot, Vice President Johnson is now president." Everyone was so upset that Miss Frommer did not scold me. Poor teacher, she had a roomful of crying young women and trying-not-to-cry young men. She started talking about the Lincoln assassination and how it spawned so many books. "The most popular book could have been called *Lincoln's Doctor's Dog*. You'll see there will be all kinds of books written about Kennedy, his life, and his assassination."

We had the pep rally early that day. I suppose Shep thought it might raise our spirits. Students weren't cheering much; mainly quietly talking. The school buses lined up out front early that day which ordinarily would have met with great jubilation. We rode home silently.

But, if you were my Uncle Louis, Kennedy wasn't dead although it was the telephone company who had tried to kill him. My Uncle Louis was married to my mother's youngest sister, and he had a conspiracy theory for every event in history. My mother would caution my father before Uncle Louis and Aunt Helen visited. "Just ignore what he says." My father had given up years before trying to reason with the man. "Don't worry. I'll just agree with him." So my dad just nodded his head "yes" as Uncle Louis talked about how Kennedy was a vegetable in a hospital in Dallas paralyzed but not killed by the phone company who feared he would nationalize them. Lee Harvey Oswald was Ma Bell's patsy.

For the longest time, he thought Roosevelt was still alive but paralyzed somewhere visited by Eleanor just as Jackie visited JFK in Dallas. Eventually, he gave up on FDR being alive and no longer talked about it, but he never lost his belief that Roosevelt knew of the Pearl Harbor attack and let it happen to get the United States into World War II.

I often wondered where Uncle Louis got these stories. He seemed perfectly normal to me on the surface, but he had a deep distrust of the government, utilities, science, education, religion, you name it. I found him entertaining in his certainty man didn't go to the moon, let alone walk on it or drive golf carts around up there—it was all staged by NASA as a diversion from the Vietnam War. Since 1948 Roswell UFO's routinely visited us and many of them were now our leaders. That made the Freemasons or Baptists or Avon ladies, whoever Uncle Louis suspected was running the world on a certain day, all aliens. Bigfoot existed, a governmental scientific experiment gone awry. Shooting rockets into the atmosphere had ruined our weather. There might be something to these last two thoughts. When anything horrendous happens, I wonder how Uncle Louis would see it if he were still alive. He would be right there with the idea that the government brought down the World Trade Center.

Everyone in the family, including Aunt Helen had developed a "live and let the conspiracies go their own way" attitude. On one visit after he and my aunt left, my dad said, "I think I made Louis mad. All I did was agree with him, but he still left mad." Uncle Louis had probably guessed there was a conspiracy not to pay any attention to anything he said.

*After a hard day in the fields, from left to right, Aunt Nellie, my mother, my father*

*Proof #10*

# FARM LIFE IS ENTERTAINING

A t the end of the evening of my high school reunion, the music started with the Beach Boys song "Surfin' USA." My classmates got up to dance in a community center in a farming town 1500 miles from the beaches of California. When the song was first popular, not one of us had been to California or knew anyone from there. "I Wanna Hold Your Hand" by The Beatles was the next song played. It had caused boys to comb their hair forward and for girls to straighten theirs 3,000 miles from Liverpool. We hadn't even heard of Liverpool until The Beatles. The world started to shrink in the late '60s, first with music. Although no one in my family was musical, we valued music. We couldn't sing or play instruments, but we could operate radios and record players. Music served as background to all the work that needed to be done on the farm.

In the final hours of the reunion, I waited in vain for a Rolling Stones tune. The party planners had asked in their questionnaire, "What was your favorite song or group from high school?" Most of my class replied with the Beach Boys. The Beatles came in second. Elvis got a lot of votes, too. I'm the only one who supported the Stones. As an aging aspiring groupie, I had followed them around with their Bigger Bang tour as much as I could the previous year. Since 1964 I attended as many of their concerts possible, waving the British Union Jack. The last time I saw the Stones in

Kansas City on their Zip Code tour, I swear I got a look from Mick Jagger that seemed to say, "After all these years, she's still there!" Sir Mick quickly turned his attention to the younger, perkier females in the crowd, but I can die happy.

If we were in the farm house, music was playing from the radio or from a portable record player that first only played 78s. Later we upgraded to a machine that played the smaller one-tune front and back 45. You could push the plastic piece down that you needed to play the 45 records, and it would play albums at 33 and 1/3 rpm. The gadget looked like a small suitcase complete with a handle so you could carry it about. As a teenager I had my own record playing console in my room, and my parents used the portable one in the kitchen or living room. For both contraptions the "diamond" needles scratched the records or skipped parts of the songs, but it was still music.

My father favored gospel and blues. My mother liked Big Band sounds of the 40s and virtuoso performers such as Liberace or opera singers like Mario Lanza. My oldest sister was in love with Andy Williams. When he built his theater in Branson, not far from where Edith lived, it caused my nephew, her son, to ponder, "I guess if she was still alive I'd have to just take her there and leave her." Now that Andy's gone, I hope Edith isn't pestering him too much in heaven. We all loved Elvis as he seemed to hit each one of our favorite types of music: ballad, classical, rock 'n roll, gospel, blues.

My mother, who was anything but frivolous, had special ordered Elvis's 45 recording of "It's Now or Never" from Carlton's Store. Elvis sang his love song to the tune of "O Sole Mio." It was the spring of 1960. Carlton's called to say that her record was in. Mom changed her clothes, even put on high heels, as if Elvis was personally going to hand it to her, and drove to the store to pick it up. She played it all day long which was no easy task as the technology demanded you had to literally go over and pick up the arm with the needle and put it down at the beginning of the record to start it over again. Every three minutes or so, she repeated the process, and Elvis began his tortured croon again. If it had been possible, she would have anxiously awaited Elvis's next tour as I anticipate the same for the Rolling Stones.

For an Iowa farm girl, I got quite an insight into the growth of music from a world stage. I saw the Beatles in St. Louis on August 21, 1966, which would turn out to be their final tour in front of a live audience. My brother-in-law bought tickets that cost him a hefty $5.00 each. It rained heavily that day at Busch Stadium. If the Cardinals had been playing baseball, the game would have been called. As this was a Beatles concert and they were scheduled to move onto the next venue, the crowd waited and waited. When a break came in the clouds around 8:30 at night, the four walked out of the bullpen, onto the plastic-covered ball diamond. They threaded past third base and climbed the steps onto the platforms as stagehands removed plastic sheets from the microphones and the drums. The screams went up, the flashbulbs went off.

I had taken my Kodak Brownie camera with a fresh roll of film. As soon as I saw the Beatles, I licked the flashbulb base to make better contact, put the bulb in the round Brownie holder, then focused, clicked and the bulb crackled. I burnt my fingers removing the hot bulb, and I started the process all over again. I put burned-out flashbulbs into my pocket as fast as I could. Not one photo came out such was the state of photography then so I had to be satisfied with the souvenir book I bought for one dollar after the show.

The Beatles looked like little dolls down on the field. John Lennon in his bow-legged stance rhythmically moved up and down. Paul played his guitar with his left hand, Ringo flopped his hair side to side as he played the drums, and George was George. When they were finished most of the crowd screamed, jumped up and left as the Beatles departed the arena. The warm-up entertainers now took the stage. The rain had resumed lightly and the Ronettes had to sing "Be My Baby" in the drizzle with Ronnie holding a plastic rain cap, one of those with of accordion folds you could easily store in your pocket, over her head. The Cyrkle, a group of Americans also handled by the Beatles manager Brian Epstein, did their hit "Red Rubber Ball" which was all about surviving a breakup. The dumped sees that life is going to be all right as the sun has come up like, you guessed, that bouncy ball.

I saw the Beatles in their last live tour before an American audience and the Rolling Stones in their first tour of the United States. After the Beatles came to the United States in February 1964, the gates were open for the "British Invasion" of all types of English groups onto the American record charts. The names alone were inventive: The Moody Blues, The Who, The Hollies. Then there were all the "and" groups: Billy J. Kramer AND the Dakotas, Gerry AND the Pacemakers, Freddie AND the Dreamers, which I suppose gave rise to the American group, Paul Revere AND the Raiders. On both sides of the Atlantic were groups of single word names, often misspelled, with origins in nature: Yardbirds, Zombies, Monkees, Turtles.

My friend Katie's older sister, Nancy, had gone to work in the Big City in the extremely glamorous position as a secretary at a television station. Katie called me on a Saturday morning, June 13, 1964. Did I want to go with her to see the local dance show that afternoon hosted by Boogie Bob? Nancy's boss had delegated the job of finding some warm bodies to sit in the stands and clap for whatever rock group needed to promote a record or a gig. Bob could usually only snag local groups who had their origins in school assemblies. The Beach Boys had been his biggest stars.

"There's some English group called The Rolling Stones," said Katie. "No one has heard of them, but they have an album coming out. They're playing the Auditorium tonight. Nancy's job is on the line. Mom is driving, and we're also taking my cousins Pam and Sam." Pamela and Samantha were the first twins I had ever known. Together, you could tell them apart. Separately, good luck. One was smiling, the other sullen. One liked dressing up, the other didn't. That would seem enough to differentiate the two, but they were fond of taking on each other's personas. The happy, well-dressed Pam often wore jeans and scowled. Vice versa for Sam.

After Katie's mother talked with my mother, it was set. I would have rather seen the Beatles at that point, but seeing anyone from a foreign country, let alone musicians from England, was equally thrilling to me. "Rolling Stones?" my dad said. "I think that's in an old blues song."

A trip to the Big City from our farm was a rare and joyous occasion and a major journey of several hours that involved taking a packed lunch. A highlight would be stopping at a gas station and getting a bottle of soda pop from a cooler. You had to propel your bottle through a maze, put your quarter in the slot and release your bottle with an upward pull.

Katie's mother knew the way to the television station as she had visited there before. Nancy was on the sidewalk accosting anyone who passed by to come into the studio. She was so happy to see us that she almost cried. "You could only get four?! The show starts soon. We'll move one set of the bleachers out and make sure the camera just takes tight shots of the audience." I was impressed with her knowledge of television jargon. We "only four" plus Nancy which made five took our place in the stands. It looked as if everyone had called upon daughters, sisters, cousins to make an audience of around twenty. Someone with headphones and a clip board stood before us. "We have to practice screaming. Let me hear you scream." I laughed. He scowled at me. "When I point at you— scream like you're really happy." We all screamed happily except Pam or was it Sam?

Standing on a foot high, round stage were five young men unlike the Beatles in clothes that did not match and much longer hair. They sang their first American single "Not Fade Away." Mick Jagger, then as now, moved like a hummingbird on speed. His clapping hands next to his face and doing a sliding dance sideways were the main moves of his repertoire.

As they sang, we were periodically pointed at and we screamed in response which seemed to unnerve the band. When the song ended, Boogie Bob went to interview the group. "Tell us about your concert tonight," he said to Keith Richards. The first words of wisdom I ever heard from the oracle: "I would if I knew where I was." It wasn't drugs, sex or rock'n roll that made him say that. I'm sure he and the others honestly didn't know where they were. They were only in the States for about two weeks, and they were playing all over the country. Many English, including my husband, were about to learn that the United States is a very big place, and England is rather small, at least geographically.

One of the show's sponsors was a local car dealership, and they had a convertible parked next to the stage for Bob to do the commercial. One by one, following Jagger, the Stones went to the sports car to look it over. They climbed into the car. Bob trying to keep his pompadour hairdo cool strolled over to the car and took the keys out of it. As he looked at the camera he intoned, "We'll be right back after these words from our sponsors." I don't know if the viewing audience heard him say it, but the studio audience heard it: "Don't leave me here alone with the Rolling Stones."

After that, I never left the Stones. I had been schooled at my father's knee on the blues, and they were celebrating it. I wish I could have attended their concert that night. We were offered tickets, but it had not been prearranged with my mother to stay overnight from home in the Big City even with neighbors. I had to be content with putting a photo of the group inside my locker door at school.

How capricious life is. Two of the Beatles are dead as are two of the original Beach Boys and the survivors have formed their own separate bands now populated by the Beach old Boys survivors. They and the Hollies, just like Andy Williams, have played Branson just down the road from me. The town known as "Jurassic Park" for its popularity with the senior crowd also houses lots of Elvis imitators and even Beatles imitators. And the Stones still play the world. If the Stones ever built a theater in Branson (and in the depth of my soul I know they never would), my nephew could just take me there and leave me. It wouldn't be for the sex or drugs but the rock 'n roll. I would stand in the audience with my Union Jack and a sign that says "Remember Omaha 1964?"

As important as music was as a entertaining diversion from the hardships of farm life, so was hearing stories from my parents, aunts and uncles. Many of which I've put into this book. The best storyteller who first inspired the love of narrative and creativity in me was my Aunt Nellie. I hope everyone has had or will have an Aunt Nellie. Aunts have all the familiarity of being a mother without all the expectations of a mother. Their only purpose, if they choose, is to entertain you, be there for you. They love you with abandon because they know your mother has to deal with all the really serious stuff.

Aunt Nellie was my mother's sister. They were Irish twins, barely a year apart, and many people thought they were twins. Aunt Nellie was taller than my mother with all of my mother's good humor but not the capacity for laying guilt trips to keep me in line. My mother and Aunt Nellie were very close. They only lived a few miles apart yet they saw each other just about every day and talked on the phone several times a day.

Her husband, my uncle, was not the farmer my dad was. They eked out a living on a much smaller farm. Uncle Elmer disappeared from time to time into Nebraska where he could drink for a few days and then shamefully come home. Aunt Nellie stayed with us when Uncle Elmer was on one of his trips. Sometimes I stayed with them just because my parents wanted me out of the house or just for the fun of it because I could stay up as late as I liked and could eat anything I wanted. If I wanted cake for supper, not a problem. If my aunt and uncle were watching a late night Western, I could stay up to see the thrilling conclusion.

I loved Aunt Nellie's tornado stories. I still can't resist a tornado special on the Weather Channel today. In flat western Iowa we saw tornadoes and sometimes suffered because of them. From Aunt Nellie's stories, it seems that she had lived through just about every tornado to ever hit the Midwest. "There was this tornado, Reese Ann. It was so powerful that it drove straw through trees. It picked up all the furniture in the house and put it in South Dakota in the same order as it had been in the living room!" These were some badass tornadoes she told me about. They were always picking up people, cows, horses and planting them in other states. They pulled feathers out of chickens and sheared sheep. They could strip the clothes right off you and put them on another person as she had supposedly witnessed with a father and son. "There was the boy in his too big dad's clothes and the father was in pants up to his knees and a shirt too small!"

Her other specialty was "how to" stories of how things got named. She encouraged me to make up my own stories about these. "'Omaha' was named when a pioneer mother told her son a joke. The boy laughed, 'O Ma Ha' and on that very spot the city was founded," said Aunt Nellie. Not to be outdone, my story was about two settlers one leaving to go out west. He said to the other pioneer, "I away" and that's how "Iowa got its name." You can figure out how Ar-kan-sas or Wash-ing-ton came about on your own.

Aunt Nellie was always entering her poems in contests she found in newspapers or the back of movie star gossip magazines. She encouraged me to make up my own verses. I extended these poems to coming up with inventive graces before supper. Aunt Nellie laughed when I prayed, "Here we sit in this little townie about to eat our steak and brownie." It did not go over so well at home.

She wrote out her stories in longhand and sent them off to magazines. She authored a novel called *Hell's Hotel* about the year she spent working as a maid in a boarding house. The title was more salacious than her actual adventures there, but she wrote of lodgers playing strip poker and a railroad worker who was always flirting with her. She was the only one of my mother's sisters who had a career outside of farming before she married.

The county seat held the area's only movie theater. Going to the movies was a rare entertainment treat usually reserved for rainy days or wintertime when you couldn't work in the fields and other chores were caught up. A movie would run from Sunday through Wednesday. The selections would change Thursday through Saturday. If you wanted to see something, you had to act quickly unless it was a real blockbuster like a Disney movie. Going to a matinee or evening performance took some time. You were shown a newsreel and several cartoons usually with Bugs Bunny, Daffy Duck or Road Runner. The "B" movie would follow. It was a movie with unknown actors who wanted to be stars one day. Everyone really went to see the "A" movie. That was the one with the real movie stars.

My mother preferred Biblical epics. Aunt Nellie would attend those because she would watch anything, but her preference was for more fluff: musicals, love stories, mysteries. She liked stars in her movies and one of the biggest at the time was Elizabeth Taylor. Aunt Nellie couldn't wait for *Suddenly Last Summer* to come to the Broadway Theater. It not only had Liz but also Katherine Hepburn and Montgomery Clift. It was based on the Tennessee Williams play that had played on the real Broadway in New York. Now it would come to its namesake movie theater in western Iowa.

After the movie my mother made one comment: "If I had known what that movie was about, I never would have let Reese Ann see it." Aunt Nellie's retort was, "It beats all those Bible orgy movies you make her watch." I was only ten at the time, and it was all over my head except for how pretty Elizabeth Taylor was and how strict Katherine Hepburn was and how miserable Montgomery Clift seemed to be. I didn't understand the plot until I read the play in college. I'm not so sure that my mother and my aunt realized it involved a woman who would rather lobotomize a girl than to accept that her son liked to frolic with young men on the beach. I also never understood the Bible epics. The climax would always be a lot of people gyrating around some type of golden idol until God got really mad.

It caused a brief riff between my mother and my aunt. Aunt Nellie would call and my mother wouldn't answer the phone. At least I think it was Aunt Nellie as you couldn't tell then who was calling you in 1959. Finally, Aunt Nellie came over, and they had a tearful reunion in the driveway. Ah, farm life taught me the power of literature, cinema, and telling stories. After that our film entertainment was limited to beach movies and Elvis movies which also involved beaches and gyrating.

My English husband didn't get to know my mother or what it was like to have a mother-in-law. By the time he came along, she was very sick and died before we were married, but he did get to know my Aunt Nellie and a little bit about the time and place that made me what I am and still am, a farmer's daughter.

He experienced a typical Aunt Nellie day. We started out picking strawberries from the garden. "Strawberries hide. If only they would say, 'Here I am!' They would be so much easier to pick." After strawberry picking, she rode her horse telling us, "I rode horses even when I was pregnant with both Doug and Shirley. Doug was her son who had married and given

Aunt Nellie some grandchildren to love. Her daughter had died young. It seemed to be the only tragedy in Aunt Nellie's life except for my uncle's occasional trips. After horse back riding, we did some target shooting and then went fishing complete with digging up our own worms. It was a full day, which ended with fried chicken and strawberries for dessert. I could tell my husband loved it. Later Aunt Nellie said to me, "I couldn't understand a thing he said so I just smiled." Finding fun and smiling through was pretty much her mission statement in life. As my mother often repeated, "Nellie is always into something." I hope my nieces and nephews will say the same of me.

—w—

When we realized that there would be no Stones songs at the end of the reunion evening, we were both ready to leave. My husband's curiosity had been sated, and I wanted to return to the present. I had survived high school for a second time, very well, thank you. Twist my arm, but I'm glad I went. My high school reunion made me realize I was still a farmer's daughter. My background has served me well, and I wouldn't trade it for anything. On the farm I learned all that matters to me in life—love, work, education, fun and a hundred other lessons I keep recalling such as the perpetual habit of rising at 5:00 am for no special reason. Farm life prepared me for my next big adventure after graduation. I was going to England.

I bet you're wondering how I went from being a farmer's daughter to experiencing the life of a British bird. Well, that's another story.

*My father's three daughters who were supposed to be sons, around the time of my high school graduation. From left to right, Janyce, your author, and Edith.*

*An aerial view of the family farm.*

# About the Author

Resa Willis is a Professor Emeritus of English at Drury University in Springfield, Missouri. She is the author of *Mark and Livy, the Love Story of Mark Twain and the Woman Who Almost Tamed Him*, based on the marriage of Mark Twain and Olivia Langdon Clemens, and *FDR and Lucy: Lovers and Friends*, which explores the relationship of President Franklin Roosevelt and Lucy Mercer Rutherfurd.

A popular speaker, she has lectured across the U.S. and in England.